JOSIP BROZ TITO

JOSIP BROZ

FITZROY MACLEAN

TITO

A PICTORIAL BIOGRAPHY

A McGraw-Hill Co-Publication

Copyright © 1980 by McGraw-Hill
Book Company (UK) Limited, Maidenhead,
England. All rights reserved. No part of this
publication may be reproduced, stored in a
retrieval system, or transmitted in any form or
by any means, electronic, mechanical, photo-
copying, recording, or otherwise, without the
prior written permission of the publisher.

First published in the United Kingdom by
MACMILLAN LONDON LIMITED
London and Basingstoke
Associated companies in Delhi, Dublin,
Hong Kong, Johannesburg, Lagos, Melbourne,
New York, Singapore & Tokyo

ISBN 0-333-31003-9

Design by:
EMIL BÜHRER

Editor:
DAVID BAKER

Managing Editor:
FRANCINE PEETERS

Production Manager:
FRANZ GISLER

Printed by:
POLYGRAPHISCHE GESELLSCHAFT, LAUPEN

Bound by:
SCHUMACHER AG, SCHMITTEN

Composition by:
FEBEL AG, BASEL

Photolithography by:
PHOTOLITHO RÄSS, BERN

Printed in Switzerland

CONTENTS

Experts do not usually
take sufficient account
of the strength of the human
will.
If human beings
are really determined
to do something,
they will do it,
even if all calculation shows it
to be impossible. Tito, April 1943

Filip Filipović's gesture of defiance became a symbol of Yugoslav resistance. After the war it was celebrated by a statue at Valjevo.
His last call, just before he was hanged on the square at Valjevo, on 22 May 1942, was a cry to the people to continue the fight for freedom.

PART I

RISE
OF A
REVOLUTIONARY

The village of Kumrovec.

The earliest document in which the Broz family is mentioned as being in Zagorje. From it one learns that Ambrozij Broz, from the village of Volovja, district of Jastrebarsko, settled in 1554, as a freeman, on the biggest feudal estate in Croatia, Cesargrad.

Josip Broz, later to become famous as Marshal Tito of Yugoslavia, was born in May 1892 in the village of Kumrovec in Croatia, then part of the Austro-Hungarian Empire. He was the son of Franjo Broz, a dark-haired, easygoing peasant with a taste for drink, whose family had farmed a few nearby fields for several hundred years, and of his wife Marija, fair-haired, blue-eyed and upstanding, from neighboring Slovenia. Little Josip was the seventh of fifteen children, eight of whom died

6

Right: *The little farming village of Kumrovec, Tito's birthplace and first home, is part of the spare and hilly region of Zagorje, north of Zagreb. Cramped fields, vineyards, and orchards cling close to the steep valleys. The life and landscape of this area have hardly changed since the young Josip Broz toiled at the grueling tasks of the small farmer in his father's fields.*

in childhood. Franjo and Marija lived with some cousins in a low, solidly built, whitewashed house. Each family occupied two rooms, sharing the kitchen. Life was hard. There was often not enough to eat and even the small children worked in the fields. On Sundays Marija, a devout Catholic, would take them to the little white church of St. Roko above the village. From the age of eight Josip or Joža, a bright, lively child, attended the village school, where his marks were good. Kumrovec lay on the banks of the River Sutla in the Zagorje or Land Beyond the Mountains on the borders of Slovenia, green, hilly country full of mountain streams. Its people were Croats, speaking their own Slav language and clinging to their own ancient traditions, who from time to time had rebelled against their Austrian and Hungarian rulers much as further

south their fellow-Slavs, the Serbs, had rebelled against the Turks. On a hill nearby stood Cesargrad, the ruined castle of the Hungarian Erdödys, once feudal lords of Kumrovec.

It had been Franjo's intention to send Josip to seek his fortune in America, but when it came to the point, the money for his passage could not be found and in 1907, at fifteen, he was despatched to the nearby town of Sisak to work as a waiter in a cafe frequented by the officers of the local garrison. But a waiter's life did not suit young Josip and before long he managed to get himself a job as an apprentice in the workshop of Nicholas Karas, locksmith and general mechanic. Josip enjoyed his three years as an apprentice. He liked making things and to this day a fine wrought iron handrail he made still adorns the District Court at Sisak. He ate well. He had

Josip Broz's birthplace, his father's house in Kumrovec (right).

Franjo Broz, as his sons remember him, was a lean man with black, curly hair and an aquiline nose, "a true Dinaric type." He was born on 25 September 1856, and when he was twenty-three married a sixteen-year-old Slovene girl, Marija-Micika Javoršak, the daughter of Martin Javoršak, born in 1864 in the village of Podsreda, on the opposite side of the River Sutla.

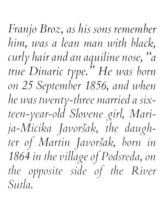

In 1907 the fifteen-year-old Josip Broz followed the advice of his cousin, Sergeant Jurica Broz, and left his village to seek work in the garrison town of Sisak, southwest of Zagreb. His first wages were earned as an assistant waiter in a restaurant that catered mainly to officers and non-commissioned officers.

In the District Court at Sisak (left) can be found the wrought-iron handrail made by Josip Broz as the completion of his apprenticeship (below). For, realizing that there was no living to be made as a waiter, Broz decided to learn a trade. Through friends he found work as an apprentice with a locksmith and mechanic named Karas. Together with the other apprentices, he lived and worked for three years in Karas' workshop, and was reportedly industrious, skillful, and carefree.

The workshop is today a museum (left), fully equipped with furnace, anvil, bellows, and all the necessary tools. On the wall hangs a replica of the wrought-iron handrail.

plenty of friends. At night-school he acquired a taste for reading and was soon devouring every book he could lay hands on.

At eighteen Broz was a trained mechanic. He wanted to get on and wanted to see the world. In 1910 he left Sisak for trained, Josip Broz made a good soldier and was soon promoted *Stabsfeldwebel* in the Croat infantry regiment in which he was serving. Nor was it long before he had the chance to prove his value as a fighter.

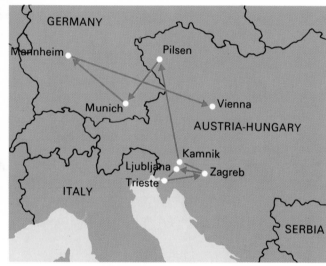

Agram or Zagreb, the capital of Croatia, where he spent two months. It was the first time he had been in a big city. With his savings he bought a fine new suit and hung it in his lodgings. But someone stole it and when he went back to Kumrovec for Christmas, he was no better dressed than anyone else.

After two months at home working as laborer, Josip set out again in search of work worthier of a trained apprentice. During the next two years he traveled over much of Austria-Hungary and Germany. The life of a *Handwerksbursch*, or journeyman, was not easy. Often he went hungry and slept in barns. But his travels taught him a lot. In his spare time he improved his knowledge of engineering, learned Czech and German, and even took dancing lessons. When, in 1913, he was called up for two years' service in the Austrian army, he was already a skilled mechanic. Country bred and town

This existence as a wandering journeyman began in 1910, when he was eighteen. Immediately on completing his apprenticeship he left Sisak and traveled to Zagreb, where a colleague from Karas' smithy helped him to find a job. Zagreb was his first encounter with city life, and with politics. He joined the Metalworkers' Union and the Social Democratic Party of Croatia and Slovenia. This continuing travel brought him, after a short visit to his parents in January 1911, to Ljubljana, where he was unable to find work, and from there to Trieste, where he was equally unsuccessful.

Returning via Zagreb, he went on to Kamnik, then traveled to Pilsen, Munich, and Mannheim, ending up in October 1912 in Vienna, where he found work at the Daimler-Benz factory. His travels brought him valuable experience, including a knowledge of Czech and German, and greater self-assurance.

The Archduke Franz Ferdinand, heir to the Imperial throne, with his wife and son.

Below: The Archduke Franz Ferdinand is greeted by the mayor of Sarajevo a few minutes before his assassination.

Below right: The Archduke's assassin, Gavrilo Princip, is seized by police and onlookers.

On 28 June 1914, while visiting Sarajevo in Bosnia, the Archduke Franz Ferdinand of Austria, heir to the old Emperor Franz-Josef, was shot dead by Gavrilo Princip, a young Bosnian Serb. The assassination, which vividly expressed the national aspirations of the emperor's South Slav subjects, had been planned in Serbia. Glad of a pretext for settling with the Serbs, the Austrian Government issued a stiff ultimatum. Russia supported Serbia. Germany backed Austria. France and Great Britain mobilized. By the beginning of August Europe was at war.

As a Slav, Josip Broz had no particular feelings of loyalty for Austria-Hungary, but, like millions of others, he obeyed orders. In the late autumn of 1914 his regiment was sent to the Carpathian front to halt the advance of the Russian armies, now within a hundred and twenty-five miles of Budapest. The weather was cold. Both sides were badly equipped. There was much heavy fighting and many casualties.

Brave, resolute, and resourceful, Broz proved a natural leader.

Night after night that winter he would take his platoon on raids and reconnaissances, bringing back prisoners and information. A snapshot taken by a friend in the trenches shows a face that is already formidable. The eyes that look along the rifle barrel are alert, the mouth determined, the expression stern and concentrated.

In Germany, as elsewhere, the outbreak of war is greeted with enthusiasm by soldiers and civilians alike. It was generally assumed—on both sides—that the armies would be coming home, victorious, within a few weeks. That the jubilant soldiers were marching off to a bloody and destructive war of catastrophic proportions occurred to hardly anyone.

Easter morning 1915 found Josip Broz and his regiment entrenched near a tributary of the Dniester. At first light they were overrun by some squadrons of Russian cavalry wearing the high black sheepskin hats and carrying the two-pronged lances of the Circassian *Dikhaya Divisia*, who had crossed the river during the night and now suddenly swept down on them, dealing death and destruction. As Broz was fighting off one Circassian with his bayonet, another ran him through the back, leaving him bleeding and unconscious. But somehow he survived and, with other prisoners, was carried back to base

and thence by stages to Russia and the little town of Sviazhesk on the Volga, where he spent the next year recovering from his wounds in hospital in an old Orthodox monastery.

When in May 1916 he was well enough to leave hospital, he was sent to Ardatov near Samara to work as a mechanic in a mill. Thence he was moved to Kungur in the Urals and put in charge of a gang of his fellow-prisoners working on the Trans-Siberian Railway. It was while he was at Kungur that there came in March 1917 the news that a revolution had

broken out in Petrograd, that the czar had abdicated and power passed to a Provisional Government.

What happened in Russia, it might be argued, was of no great concern to Feldwebel Broz. But he was young and the events taking place all round him could scarcely fail to catch his imagination. For his part, he had no special liking for emperors or empires, for capitalists or capitalism. His sympathies were with those seeking to overthrow the existing order, with the revolutionaries. Enterprising as ever, he decided to make his way by one means or another to Petrograd, to the epicenter of the upheaval. Hidden among some sacks of grain on a goods train bound for the capital, he eventually reached Petrograd.

It was a critical moment in history. Lenin had returned from Switzerland. The Provisional Government were fast losing control. Power was passing to the Workers' and Soldiers' Councils and through them to the Bolsheviks, who in July organized large-scale demonstrations against the Government. Josip Broz joined the demonstrations. When they reached the railway station, they came under heavy fire from Government troops on the roof. Widespread arrests followed

In the spring of 1915 Josip Broz was wounded and taken prisoner. The lance thrust that laid him low was a nasty one. It had entered his body just below the left arm, narrowly missing his heart and leaving a deep and troublesome wound. Thus began his odyssey across Russia, which lasted until spring 1920.

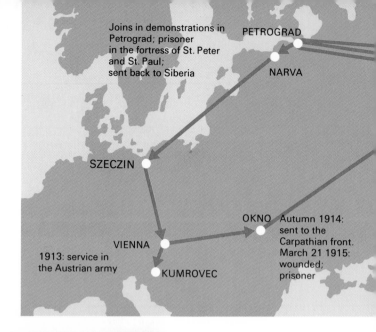

Joins in demonstrations in Petrograd; prisoner in the fortress of St. Peter and St. Paul; sent back to Siberia

PETROGRAD

NARVA

SZECZIN

OKNO — Autumn 1914: sent to the Carpathian front. March 21 1915: wounded; prisoner

VIENNA

1913: service in the Austrian army

KUMROVEC

and Broz spent three weeks in the rat-infested dungeons of the Fortress of St. Peter and St. Paul. After which he was sent back to Siberia under escort.

But Josip Broz was not an easy man to coerce. Giving his

Left: *Pelagea Byelusnova, who hid Josip Broz from the Whites and became his wife. With her is her mother.*

Below: *The house of Pelagea Byelusnova in Omsk.*

Below right: *During his flight in 1919, Josip Broz had to hide from the White Russian troops of Admiral Kolchak. He spent several months in the steppes with a band of Kirghiz nomads. He quickly won the approval of their leader, Hadji Isaj Djaksembayev, who then tried to persuade him to accept his daughter as a wife, and to remain with the tribe.*

escort the slip, he caught a passenger train to Omsk. Some days later the train was boarded by an armed mob of Bolshevik supporters, who announced that back in Petrograd the Bolsheviks had seized power. In Omsk a few days later Broz was formally enrolled in the Bolshevik Red Guard, thus becoming in the fullest sense of the word a soldier of the revolution.

He was to spend three more years in Russia, years of bloodshed and civil strife. In 1918 the Bolsheviks lost Omsk

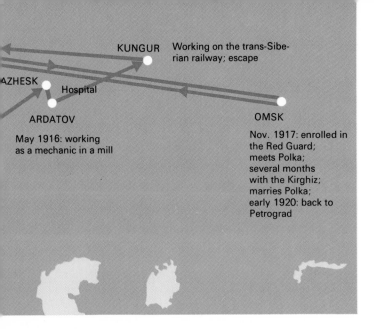

KUNGUR
Working on the trans-Siberian railway; escape

...AZHESK
Hospital

ARDATOV
May 1916: working as a mechanic in a mill

OMSK
Nov. 1917: enrolled in the Red Guard; meets Polka; several months with the Kirghiz; marries Polka; early 1920: back to Petrograd

At the end of 1919 Broz returned to Omsk, where he met Pelagea again. They were married in January 1920. Shortly after their marriage Broz decided to return home to Yugoslavia. By way of St. Petersburg, Stettin, and Vienna, he reached Kumrovec at the beginning of October.

Below: Josip Broz after his return to Yugoslavia.

to the Whites. For a time Broz was safely hidden by a beautiful fair-haired Russian girl called Pelagea or Polka Byelusnova. They fell in love, but soon he had to leave the town. In the surrounding steppes he encountered a tribe of Kirghiz nomads, whose chief, Hadji Isaj Djaksembayev, needed a mechanic for his mill. Broz spent several months with the Kirghiz. Impressed by his horsemanship, they would take him out with them spearing wolves at full gallop. Soon Hadji Isaj invited him to join the tribe and marry one of his daughters. But Broz had other plans. When, not long after, the Bolsheviks recaptured Omsk, he went back there and married Polka.

Early in 1920, taking Polka with him, he made his way, with other returning prisoners, back across a war-battered continent to his own country. When Josip Broz first came to Russia as a prisoner in 1915 he lacked any very deep convictions, any strong purpose in life. Now he had seen the Revolution triumph and the working class seize power. He had seen, or so he believed, the Future—the Future for Russia and for the whole world. He had found a cause by comparison with which family, religion, fatherland counted as nothing. He had became a Communist. Henceforth he had but one aim: to bring about a Communist revolution in his own country.

A BACKWARD GLANCE

For Josip and Polka, now pregnant, the journey home was long and difficult. It was September before they reached Kumrovec. Josip's mother had died and his father moved to another village. A few hours after their arrival Polka gave birth to a boy, but the baby died two days later. Sadly they assembled their few belongings and set out for Zagreb in search of work.

During the five years Josip Broz had spent in Russia, the old Hapsburg Empire had disintegrated. On his return he found himself a citizen of the new Kingdom of Serbs, Croats, and Slovenes, later to be renamed Yugoslavia. The creation of a Yugoslav or South Slav state was the culmination of an historical process which had begun some fourteen centuries

An artist's impression of the decisive battle between the peasants and the feudal armies on 2 February 1573 near Donja Stubica, during the peasant rebellion in Croatia and Slovenia.
The peasants fought stubbornly and courageously, and held out for four hours before being overcome by the superior equipment of the feudal cavalry.
A picture President Tito obviously cherished, since it hung behind his desk in his private office.

The strong Turkish pressure on Central Europe (1683 siege of Vienna) came to an end with Charles V of Lorraine's victory at Kahlensberg. Under the Protectorate of Pope Innocent XI Austria, Poland, Venice, and Russia formed a Holy Alliance against the Turks (1684). After the Peace of Karlowitz (1699), the capture of Belgrade (1717), and the Peace of Passarowitz (1718), Austria rose to the status of a great power.

Under pressure from Napoleon, Franz II refrained in 1806 from assuming the Imperial Crown. This signified the end of the "Holy Roman Empire of the German Nation." The settlement of the Congress of Vienna in June 1815 reasserted the balance between the five great powers (France, Great Britain, Russia, Austria, and Prussia). The tributary Principality of Serbia attained its independence through Russo-Turkish negotiations.

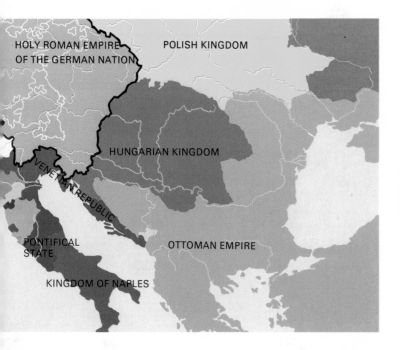

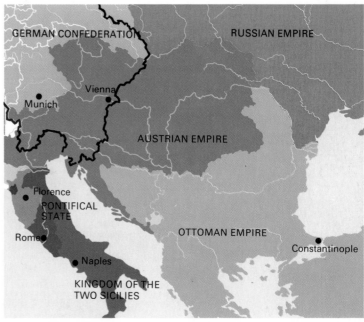

earlier when the forebears of the Slav races who now inhabit Yugoslavia first migrated there from the steppes and forests of the north.

From the start their history had been turbulent and confused, a tale of violence, heroism, and treachery, as Serb, Croat, and Slovene princes fought among themselves for supremacy, enlisting as often as not the help of this or that outside power, to attain their immediate ends. Caught between the conflicting forces of east and west, the struggle for survival was a hard one.

With time, the advance westward of the Osmanli Turks grew ever harder to check. In 1389 at Kosovo, the Field of the Blackbirds, the Serbian Czar Lazar was defeated and slain and his people passed under Turkish sway. In 1453 came the fall of Constantinople, and in 1528 the last Bosnian stronghold fell to the Turks. The whole Balkan peninsula was now under alien rule, the Turks occupying the south and east, while the Austrians and Hungarians advanced to meet them from the north and west and the Venetians established themselves along the Adriatic coast.

The old Turkish fortress of Belgrade, from Roman times a fortified site.

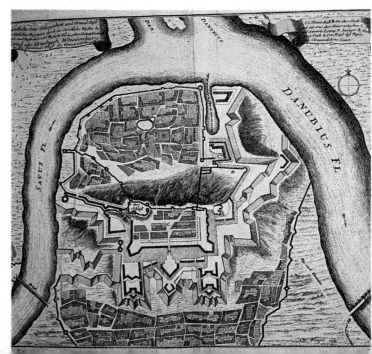

BEFORE THE FIRST WORLD WAR

The Balkans were a center of persistent unrest arising from the collapse of the Ottoman Empire, and the excessive aspirations of new nations formed across racial, cultural, and religious boundaries. This became the focal point of world politics, with the involvement directly (Austria-Hungary, Italy, Russia) or indirectly (Germany, France, Great Britain) of the great powers.

THE SECOND WORLD WAR

The "Greater German Empire," Allies and occupied areas (brown) before the Balkan expedition (6 April–1 June 1941). On 6 April Hitler opened his Balkan offensive with the air attack on Belgrade. Yugoslavia was invaded from Hungary, Bulgaria, and Roumania. The Yugoslav Army surrendered on 17 April.

In this way the South Slavs were separated, Serbia and Bosnia falling to the sultans, while Croatia and Slovenia became provinces of the Hapsburg Empire. Under Turkish rule, the Serbs came to look eastward, to Constantinople. Their Church was the Orthodox Church. The Croats and Slovenes, for their part, looked westward to Vienna, belonging to the Church of Rome and enjoying the benefits of western civilization. While Belgrade remained a Turkish fortress, Zagreb or Agram became a European city.

But the Serbs never lost their love of freedom. Over the years the spirit of independence was kept alive by little bands of guerrilla fighters, half brigands and half patriots, while in their mountain fastnesses, the neighboring Montenegrins held out unsubdued for century after century. It was thus that, when in the early nineteenth century the Ottoman Empire began to crumble, there still remained in Serbia a nucleus of resistance, ready to flare up into a national revolt.

In 1804 the Serbs, led by a peasant called Kara Djordje or Black George, rose against the Turks and within three years had driven them from Serbia. In 1809 the Turks returned, but

Black George drove them out again, this time with Russian help. In 1813 they returned once more in overwhelming force. Kara Djordje was defeated and fled abroad and the Turks appointed Miloš Obrenović, a herdsman, to govern the country for them. But in 1815 the Serbs rose yet again, led this time by Obrenović, who in a single campaign drove out the Turks and proclaimed himself Prince of Serbia. The Turks now agreed to recognize him, in return for which he accepted Turkish suzerainty. When in 1817 his rival resistance-leader, Kara Djordje, returned from exile, he cut off his head and sent it to the sultan.

For the next hundred years Serbia presents an extraordinary picture of violence, intrigue, and unrest. Rival dynasties, founded by Kara Djordje and Obrenović, served as rallying points for opposing factions. Power passed from one to the other and back again. In her struggle for nationhood, Serbia sided first with one great power and then with another, while the great powers, in turn, supported first one Serb faction and then the other.

After fighting side by side with the Russians in the Russo-

North Atlantic Treaty Organization (NATO, blue) and Warsaw Pact (red).
By the creation of the Non-Aligned group of countries, Tito assured his country of extensive friendly international relations, and was correspondingly able to relax the tension of Yugoslavia's isolated position between the Soviet Bloc and the West.

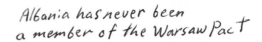

Albania has never been a member of the Warsaw Pact

whelming odds, their ultimate aim being reunion with the South Slavs of Austria-Hungary, an aim they shared with many of their South Slav brothers across the border. In December 1918, at a joint session of the Serbian Skupština and a South Slav Council set up in Zagreb, the union was ratified and Peter Karadjordjević became king of a new Triune Kingdom of Serbs, Croats, and Slovenes, including Montenegro, now united to Serbia. On his death three years later he was succeeded by his son Alexander, a stubborn, austere, courageous man with an autocratic nature and a strong, if narrow sense of duty.

The new kingdom, of which Josip Broz had willy-nilly become a citizen, was more than twice the size of the old Serbia, with a population of about twelve million, including some five million Serbs, three million Croats, and one million Slovenes. Its territories extended from the frontiers of Italy, Austria, and Hungary on the north to those of Greece and Albania on the south. To the West its coastline stretched for four hundred miles along the Adriatic. To the east it bordered with Roumania and Bulgaria. Geographically, and in other respects too, it was a land of great diversity, but by race its inhabitants were almost all South Slavs, speaking different versions of the same South Slav language and now, after many trials and tribulations, at last united in a South Slav state of their own.

And yet it was not long before there were signs that all was not well in the new state. To the Serbs it seemed only right that they should occupy a dominant position in it, that it should be ruled over by a Serbian king and governed by Serbian statesmen, that its capital should be in Belgrade, a Serbian city, that its army should be commanded by Serbs and that its national church should be the Serbian Orthodox Church. But the Croats thought otherwise, clinging tenaciously to what they regarded as their superior culture and civilization, to their links with the West and their church, the Church of Rome. To them it was a matter for resentment that their national leaders, who had played their part in the foundation of the new state, should be virtually excluded from the conduct of its affairs. By 1921 Stjepan

Turkish War of 1877, Serbia was rewarded by the grant in 1878 of her complete independence from Turkey, becoming an even greater focus of attraction for those South Slavs who remained under foreign domination and, as such, a cause of growing concern to Austria-Hungary. In 1903 things were made worse by the assassination of King Alexander Obrenović, whom the Austrians trusted, and his replacement by King Peter Karadjordjević, Black George's grandson, known for his pro-Russian and anti-Austrian proclivities. In 1908 the annexation by the Austrians of the Slav-populated Turkish provinces of Bosnia and Hercegovina, which the Serbs regarded as Serbian territory, further aggravated matters. Outraged, the Serbs compensated themselves at the expense of the Turks and Bulgars, emerging from the Balkan Wars of 1912 and 1913 with their prestige enhanced and their territory greatly enlarged. By the summer of 1914 the Austrian Government had decided it was time to eliminate the Serbian menace once and for all. The assassination of the Archduke Franz Ferdinand gave them the pretext they needed.

From 1914 to 1918 the Serbs fought bravely against over-

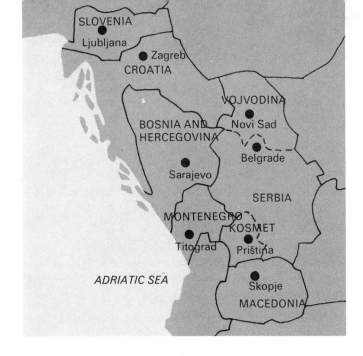

Radić, leader of the Croat Peasant Party, had come into serious conflict with the Belgrade Government and more than once been imprisoned for his pains.

Repression did not solve the Croat problem. Soon there was widespread discontent in Croatia. Nor was the Yugoslav economic situation at all reassuring. There had been widespread destruction during the war. The economy was dislocated. Corruption and profiteering were rife. Unemployment was high. Food was short. Prices were high and wages low.

Repeatedly the troops were called out to deal with strikes and disturbances.

This unrest lent grist to one mill. At its Second Congress in June 1920 the Yugoslav Socialist Workers' Party changed its name to the Communist Party of Yugoslavia. At the ensuing elections fifty-nine Communist deputies were elected to the Skupština. From the first the new party belonged to the Communist International or Comintern, its members' first loyalty being not to their own country but to Moscow, where the Comintern had its headquarters.

To Josip Broz, fresh from the country of the Revolution, this presented no problem. The new Kingdom of the Serbs, Croats, and Slovenes meant no more to him than the old Hapsburg Empire had done. His hopes, his aims, his loyalties lay elsewhere. The new party corresponded exactly to his needs and aspirations. In the autumn of 1920 he was admitted to the Zagreb Branch.

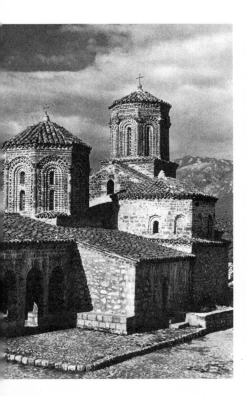

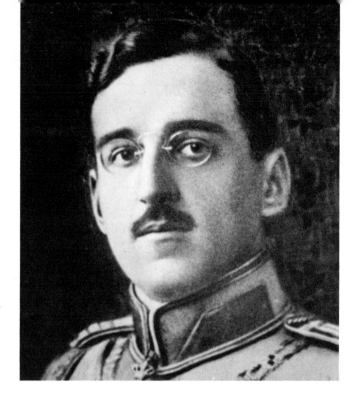

THE
NEW KINGDOM

In Zagreb Josip Broz found work in an engineering workshop and rejoined the Metalworkers' Union. He could now do what he most wanted to do and spread the new faith. His words fell on fertile ground. His fellow-workers liked him and listened to what he had to say. He spoke with burning conviction of the class struggle, of what he had seen in Russia, and of the need for the workers to seize power. That winter he helped organize a strike in Zagreb.

In the new kingdom an agitator's task was daily becoming more difficult. Warned by what had happened in Russia, the Government took drastic action against the Communists. In 1921 a law was passed making the Party illegal. Its deputies were expelled from the Skupština and its members made liable to immediate arrest. From now onward Josip Broz and his comrades were political outlaws. Nor did the Party leaders rise to this challenge, but spent more and more time abroad, arguing among themselves on points of doctrine and leaving the rank and file to fend for themselves, Josip Broz among them.

Early in 1921 Broz left Zagreb for the little village of Veliko Trojstvo, where he found employment at a flour mill belonging to a man called Samuel Polak. Polak did not worry about

his workers' political opinions, so long as they did their job. The mill was the center of village life. To the peasants who brought their grain to be ground there Broz would talk of Russia and the Revolution.

In the provinces the Party organization had been badly disrupted, but from Veliko Trojstvo Broz managed to make contact with underground cells in the nearby towns. In 1924 he was elected a member of the Regional Committee and in this capacity would from time to time visit Zagreb. Before long his activities began to attract the attention of the police. In 1924 he was denounced for a speech made at a friend's funeral and briefly imprisoned.

At Veliko Trojstvo, Josip and Polka Broz lost two more chil-

dren, a boy called Hinko who died when he was a few days old and a girl called Zlatica who lived till she was nearly two and then died of diphtheria. Sadly Broz carried her body to the graveyard in a small rough coffin a friend had made for him. When he had saved enough money, he put up a marble tombstone to the two of them. Having lost their first three children, he and Polka were overjoyed by the birth in 1924 of a sturdy, fair-haired, blue-eyed little boy, called Žarko. In the autumn of 1925 Broz moved at the behest of the Party from Veliko Trojstvo to Kraljevica, a little seaport on the northern Adriatic, where he found work building and repairing marine engines. His instructions were to organize a trade union branch and form a Party cell. He did both. Pay and working conditions at the foreign-owned shipyard were bad and what Broz had to say carried conviction. A two hours' stoppage of work was followed by a nine days' strike. Not long after, the management informed him that his services were no longer needed. But behind him he left a nucleus of industrial and political unrest. In October 1926 he moved to Smederevska Palanka, south of Belgrade, where he took a job in the railway repair workshops. Here again, he became a shop steward and again left behind him, when dismissed six months later, a flourishing Party cell. On reporting back to

Party headquarters in Zagreb, six months later, he was told that he had been chosen by the Party to be Secretary to the Zagreb branch of the Metalworkers' Union, thus becoming at thirty-five a full-time trade union official or, to put it another way, a full-time Party executive.

Below: *Newspaper cuttings concerning the shipyard at Kraljevica (left) where Broz was active in trying to improve working conditions in 1925, and (right) reporting his trial at Ogulin in 1927 on the charge of distributing subversive literature, for which he was sentenced to seven months' imprisonment.*

By this time the police were beginning to take a still keener interest in his activities. What they needed was evidence that he was an actual Party member. In the end the best they could do was to arrest him on a charge of distributing subversive literature. After four months in jail he was brought to trial in October 1927 and sentenced to seven months' imprisonment. On appealing he was released pending trial and, returning to Zagreb, resumed his trade union work. Some months later he was elected to the Central Committee of the Zagreb branch of the Party.

Early in 1928 the economic situation in Yugoslavia deteriorated sharply. The result was widespread unrest. But the Yugoslav Communist Party were in no position to take advantage of it, being badly led and strongly at variance among themselves. In seven years their membership had fallen from 60,000 to barely 3,000. Ever since 1921 they had been deeply divided over the question of the nationalities. Originally they had favored national unity. Some still clung to this view; others supported the demands of the non-Serb nationalities for self-determination. Already in 1922 the Fourth Congress of the Comintern had criticized them for "fractionalism." In 1924 the Fifth Congress had again reproved them. The Serbs, Croats, and Slovenes, the Comintern declared, were not one people, but three peoples and the Yugoslav Party must fight for the right of "self-determination to the point of secession," in other words, for the disruption of the new kingdom as an "imperialist outpost."

In 1925 and again in 1926 further Comintern resolutions criticized the Yugoslavs for fractionalism and for their failure to grasp the true significance of the question of nationalities, accusing them of "deviations to the right and deviations to the left" and declaring that, owing to sectarian strife, they "had not fulfilled a single one of their tasks."

At their Third Congress, held in Vienna in the summer of

1926, the Yugoslav Party sought belatedly to make amends, humbly admitting their disunity and other shortcomings. But even so their dissensions continued.

To a keen Party worker like Josip Broz and those who thought like him, this was deplorable. Their chance came at the Eighth Party Conference for the Zagreb area, held clandestinely in a house in the suburbs of Zagreb at the end of February 1928. Rising one after the other, they openly attacked their leaders for their failure to combat fractionalism, and demanded that a letter be sent to the Comintern condemning not one but both factions. Though in a minority, they got their way. A new Central Committee was elected and Broz appointed Branch Secretary. His first act was to send direct to the Comintern a letter urging that vigorous steps be taken to liquidate "fractional strife in the Communist Party of Yugoslavia." In Moscow neither the letter nor its author passed unnoticed. A few weeks later the Executive Committee of the Comintern responded with an "open letter" once again calling on the Yugoslav Communist Party to put an end to fractional strife. At the same time the old leadership of the Party was swept away and a new Central Committee appointed, formal effect being given to these changes at the Fourth Party Congress, held in Dresden in October 1928, which marked the Yugoslav Party's final subordination to the Communist International.

Josip Broz did not attend the Dresden Conference. In Yugoslavia there was now widespread unrest and as Party Secretary for Zagreb he had been busier than ever, preparing for what began to look like a revolutionary situation. The crisis came to a head when on 20 June 1928 during a debate in the Skupština a Government supporter drew his pistol and opened fire on the Opposition benches, mortally wounding Stjepan Radić and killing two other members of the Croat Peasant Party. In Zagreb serious rioting broke out in which the Communists joined enthusiastically.

In 1928 the police were again able to arrest Broz, who was living "illegally." He spent three months in jail. Then, from November 6 to 14, in the Zagreb Court of Justice, Josip Broz was tried and sentenced to five years' imprisonment. During the trial he said, speaking about the class terror of the bourgeoisie:
"I believe that natural laws are higher than those created by one class to oppress another. I am even prepared to sacrifice my life for my ideals...."

Below left: *Josip Broz and Moša Pijade first made friends in jail. Broz found Moša a stimulating companion.*

Below right: *Josip Broz, from a sketch made at his trial, which was fully reported in the press.*

By this time the police were searching everywhere for Broz, who was now living "illegally," using a variety of false names and disguises and keeping constantly on the move. He had some close shaves. Once the police came upon him at the headquarters of the Metalworkers' Union. "Is Josip Broz here?" they asked. "Can't you see he isn't?" he replied. On another occasion he only escaped arrest by jumping out of the window.

In the end, however, the police caught up with him. Lured by a provocateur to a room where he and other Party members occasionally spent the night, he was seized as he entered

I have proclaimed the injustice suffered by the proletariat at the hands of a bourgeois government. I admit that I have expressed that idea in public and in private ever since the Communist Party ceased to be legal and became illegal. But I do not recognize your bourgeois court of justice. I consider myself responsible only to my own Party."

The proceedings concluded on 9 November when the public prosecutor called for a heavy sentence. It had been Broz's intention to make a speech in reply, telling of all the oppression and injustice there was in the world and of the part the Communist Party would play in putting all this to rights. But

the room by two plain-clothes policemen. This time serious charges were brought against him: membership of the Party, spreading Communist propaganda, the illegal possession of bombs and firearms. After three months in prison, he came up for trial at Zagreb with five associates on 6 November 1928. The trial was widely reported in the press. The correspondent of *Novosti* was struck by the way in which he dominated the proceedings. "His," he wrote, "is undoubtedly the most interesting personality in this trial. His face makes you think of steel. His light gray eyes, behind his spectacles, are cold, but alert and calm."

From the start he took the offensive. "I admit," he said, "that I am a member of the illegal Communist Party of Yugoslavia. I admit that I have spread Communist propaganda and that

no sooner had he started than the president of the court ruled him out of order, whereupon Broz jumped up and shouted: "What better proof could there be that this is a police state? Long live the Communist Party! Long live the World Revolution!" The sentences were announced on November 14. Broz was sentenced to five years and five months in prison. After the sentences had been read out he again shouted out at the top of his voice: "Long live the Communist Party! Long live the Third International!"

All this was fully reported in the press and to many people Broz became a hero. Had he acted differently at the trial, he might have been given a shorter sentence. "But," he said afterward, "our Party needed showing that it was a proud thing to be a Communist."

Broz served most of his sentence at Lepoglava, not far from his own Zagorje. In prison he was put in charge of the power plant and in return for this was allowed books to read and other privileges, including comparative freedom of movement. Before long he had started a Communist Party organization in the prison and even established contact with his comrades in Zagreb.

In jail with Josip Broz was a Jewish intellectual from Belgrade called Moša Pijade, an odd-looking little man with spectacles and a small mustache, who was serving a fourteen-year sentence for disseminating Communist propaganda. Soon he and

In the courtyard of Lepoglava prison, where Josip Broz spent five years of his life. A group portrait of prisoners and guards.

Below left: The cell in Lepoglava occupied by Prisoner No. 483, Broz, Josip.

Below middle: Josip Broz in the prison power station, which he looked after, together with Moša Pijade.

Below right: Josip Broz (center) with two fellow prisoners.

Broz became friends. Broz found Moša fascinating to talk to, while Moša was struck by the directness and pertinence of the questions Broz asked during their discussions on Communist theory. Broz used his years in prison to continue and complete his modest early education. At last he had leisure to read extensively, talking it all over afterward with Moša and his other fellow-prisoners. "It was," he once said to the present author, "just like being at a university."

On his release from jail in March 1934 Broz was instructed by the police to remain at Kumrovec and report daily to the authorities. Putting on a smart new suit, he set out for Kumrovec.

and established what was in effect a personal dictatorship. These had been bad years for the Yugoslav Communist Party. Out of barely three thousand members the police had in two years succeeded in arresting a thousand and killing a hundred. As the Central Committee put it in their report to the Fifth Party Congress, "Party life in the country died down in 1930 and 1931. Only scattered groups survived. Almost all the leading Party cadres, at both a high and low level, were in jail, had been killed, or had emigrated." From the safety of Vienna, where they had taken refuge, the Party leaders sent confused instructions to what remained of the rank and file.

Like the Communists, the Croat Peasant Party suffered their

Far left: *The assassination of King Alexander in Marseilles on 9 October 1934. The murder was planned and carried out by the nationalist Croat terrorist organization Ustaša, led by the notorious Dr. Ante Pavelić.*

Left: *Crown Prince Peter, still in his minority at the time of his father's death. He was declared of age when Prince Paul was overthrown and, as king, emigrated to London with his government a few days after the war started.*

A lot had happened during the years which Josip Broz spent in prison. In 1929 the slump had hit the United States. In 1931 war had broken out in the Far East. In 1933 Hitler had come to power in Germany. In Yugoslavia things had come to a head on 6 January 1929, when King Alexander, having failed to reach a working agreement with the Croat Peasant Party, had simply suspended the constitution, dissolved parliament,

full share of persecution. In Zagreb meanwhile a number of the more extreme Croat nationalists had formed a secret organization known as the Ustaša or rebels, whose avowed aim was the establishment of an independent State of Croatia. As their *Poglavnik* or leader they chose Dr. Ante Pavelić, a lawyer and former member of the Skupština who, with the support of the Italian and Hungarian Governments, both enemies of Yugoslavia, now set up in Italy and Hungary centers where Ustaša agents could be specially trained and equipped before being sent back to Yugoslavia to commit acts of terrorism. One of their prime targets was King Alexander. "You may hide yourself, you gipsy," declared Dr. Pavelić in a broadsheet, "but wherever you go, we will find you and kill you."

After a short visit to Kumrovec Broz went underground. His parents were both dead. While he was in jail, his wife and child had been sent by the Party to Russia. Making his way to Zagreb, he reestablished contact with the local Party organization. The police had issued a warrant for his arrest. But he was not an easy man to catch. His life from now onward was that of a professional revolutionary.

At forty-two his devotion to the Communist cause was stronger than ever. He had lost none of his old energy and decisiveness. He was better educated, more thoughtful and more mature, in short well fitted in every way for the increasingly important role that he was henceforth to assume.

In Zagreb, where his conduct at his trial was still remembered, he was at once elected a member of the Party's new Provincial Committee for Croatia. Their problem was to establish regular contact with the Central Committee of the Party in Vienna. It was decided that Broz should go there to discuss the best method of establishing regular communications. Having provided himself with a stout pair of boots, a rucksack, and a card showing him to be a member of the Mountaineering Club of Slovenia, he accordingly set out on foot across the mountains and, avoiding the regular frontier posts, reached Klagenfurt. Thence he caught a train to Vienna, where in due course he established contact with the Central Committee.

Milan Gorkić, at this time Secretary of the Yugoslav Communist Party, was a large red-haired man with freckles who had been appointed to the post two years earlier, after one of the Comintern's periodical purges. Before that he had spent twelve years or so working at Comintern headquarters in Moscow. He and the other members of the Central Committee seemed glad to see Broz, falling on him, as he put it "like bees on honey." He, for his part, gave them a frank account of conditions in Yugoslavia and of the frame of mind of the Party there. The rank and file, he said, disliked having absentee leaders. After some discussion he was told that he had been coopted to the Central Committee and might now regard himself as one of the Leaders of the Party. As such, he was to return to Yugoslavia and try to hold Party Conferences first for Croatia and Slovenia and then for the whole country. With this directive he returned in August to Zagreb and at once got down to work. In September Party conferences were duly held in Croatia and Slovenia and full reports despatched to Vienna.

One of Broz's aims was to collect round him a nucleus of active Party members capable of putting new life into the run-down Party machine. In Slovenia he met Edvard Kardelj, a short, dark, reserved young schoolteacher, now in his twenties, with spectacles and a slight limp. At nineteen he had been caught by the police and badly tortured but had revealed nothing. Broz was struck by his steadfastness, his efficiency, and his calm, equable temperament. Then there was Boris Kidrič, the son of a professor at Ljubljana University, another promising young man.

Kardelj and his friends were no less impressed by Josip Broz. "We found him," he said, "very direct of speech and manner. He was in his early forties, about twenty years older than we were, and looked it. But he was nothing like the old Party leaders. When you asked him a question, he didn't always come back at you with a quotation from Marx, Engels, or Lenin. Instead, he spoke in practical, common-sense terms. 'This,' he would say, 'is the problem we are facing. This is what I think ought to be done. Do any of you think differently?'"

Toward the end of September Broz went back to Vienna to report, after which he returned to Yugoslavia. He had not been there for more than a few days when news was received of the assassination in Marseilles of King Alexander of Yugoslavia by an Ustaša killer. In Yugoslavia drastic security measures were now introduced which made life there more dangerous than ever for Josip Broz. Of late he had proved of value to the Party. He was accordingly instructed to return at once to Vienna en route for the Soviet Union. On Christmas Day 1934, just before he left, the Fourth Party Conference, for which he had been preparing, was secretly held in a flat in Ljubljana and a new Central Committee elected of which he himself became a member and also a member of the Party's Politburo. A few days later he left for Moscow, traveling, as usual, clandestinely.

Much had happened in Russia since Josip Broz had left it in 1920. In 1924 Lenin had died. Already during his last illness, the struggle for the succession had begun between Stalin and Trotski, ending five years later in victory for Stalin and the downfall and exile of Trotski. Thereafter Stalin had turned his formidable energies to the gigantic task of modernizing, industrializing, and arming a still backward agricultural country, while at the same time consolidating his own personal power by any and every means.

By 1935 he could claim to have made good progress on both counts. At enormous cost in human lives and suffering, Soviet agriculture had been collectivized and Soviet industry launched on the first of a series of Five Year Plans, while, as the war clouds gathered over Europe, the Red Army gradually acquired the characteristics of a modern military machine. Meantime the Soviet state, far from withering away, as Marx had said it should, was growing daily more powerful, while Stalin, through the Party and an ubiquitous, eternally watchful secret police, himself exercised total control over the state. All this in the name of Socialism in One Country, while Trotski's wider concept of World Revolution was, for the time being, relegated to the realms of theory. In Russia much remained as it had been, not fifteen, but a hundred and fifty years before. But for Josip Broz, regarding the Soviet scene with the eye of faith, there were enough signs of progress and change to convince him that it had all been worthwhile, that his own efforts and the efforts of millions of other revolutionaries had not been wasted, that this, whatever its detractors might say, was still the Country of the Revolution.

To Josip Broz, as to any other returning Communist, this resumption of contact with the source and repository of all revolutionary wisdom and grace was inevitably a moment of supreme importance. It was in Russia, after all, that, as a young man, the Truth, the ultimate Truth, had been revealed to him. It was to Russia that his thoughts had turned again and again in the intervening years. And now he was back there, back in the Land of Socialism, the center of things.

Even so there were things that did not come up to his expectations. "I was excited at being back," he said to the present author many years later, "but soon my excitement began to cool off. I saw things that were quite different from what I myself had so enthusiastically described in Yugoslavia."

In January 1935, on the recommendation of the Central Committee of the Yugoslav Party Broz was appointed to the

Left: *The Hotel Lux on Moscow's Gorki Street provided quarters for many of the more important foreign Communists in the city.*

Far left: *Tito worked in the Balkan Secretariat of the Communist International, then situated on the Makhorava, across the road from the Kremlin.*

Balkan Secretariat of the Comintern as rapporteur for Yugoslavia. "Tell Valija and the rest of them," wrote Gorkić, "that he is a worker who has spent six years in prison and that perhaps at first he will not be as skillful as some of the more experienced intellectuals. But he knows the Party; he represents the best elements among our active workers; and at the end of six or eight months we intend to recall him for important work on the Central Committee." Meanwhile, for Comintern purposes he was given the name Comrade Walter.

Left: *Trotski, one of the creators of the Red Army, was in the end outmaneuvered by Stalin.*

Right: *Georgi Dimitrov, Secretary General of the Comintern.*

Wilhelm Pieck, Head of the Balkan Secretariat.

Palmiro Togliatti played an important part in the affairs of the Comintern before the war.

His office was in the rather dingy Comintern building on the Makhovaya across the road from the Kremlin. He lived at the Hotel Lux on Ulitsa Gorkovo, a musty old caravansary for foreign Communists, where he could, if he chose, rub shoulders with Togliatti, Kuusinnen, Diaz, Dimitrov, and Earl Browder. Sometimes he would eat in the restaurant downstairs and sometimes, when rubles were short, warm something up on a spirit lamp in his room. After an initial bout of sightseeing (he had never before been to Moscow), he settled down to an existence of monastic seclusion between his office and his hotel room. His marriage had broken up. Six years on her own in Moscow had been too much for Polka. The Soviet ruling class had welcomed the still attractive young woman literally with open arms and, delighted by her success and by the material and other advantages of her new existence, she had forgotten her husband in jail back in Yugoslavia and given herself up to the delights of her new life. Soon after his arrival in Moscow she obtained a divorce and married one of her protectors. In the phrase of an acquaintance, "she was swallowed up by bureaucratic society."

Broz spent much of his time alone in his room, reading. In addition to social and economic subjects, he made a special study of military science, reading Clausewitz and the Germans, as well as the Soviet theorists. Was he not, after all, a soldier of the revolution who might one day be called upon to do battle for his beliefs?

In Moscow he resumed his acquaintance with Edvard Kardelj, the quiet young schoolteacher whom he had met the previous autumn in Slovenia, now taking a course at the International School of Leninism.

In August 1935 Broz, as Secretary of the Yugoslav Delegation,

Photo of Edvard Kardelj, taken at Belgrade police headquarters in 1930. Kardelj remained throughout his life one of Tito's closest associates.

attended the Seventh Congress of the Comintern and there for the first time saw Stalin, squat and inscrutable in his plain drab tunic. For Communists the world over the Seventh Congress marked what was described as "a new tactical orientation," in other words a complete change of policy, necessitated by the stark reality of the German menace. In future there was to be a measure of cooperation by Communists with the bourgeois democratic parties under the guise of a "Popular Front against Fascism." To implement the new policy and as a symbol of the struggle against Fascism, Georgi Dimitrov, the Bulgarian hero of Hitler's notorious Reichstag fire trial, was appointed Secretary General of the Comintern.

For the Yugoslav Communists another change of line concerned the Party's policy in regard to the nationalities. The Party, it appeared, must no longer support Croat and other demands for independence in the hope of thereby disrupting the existing Yugoslav state. Revolution for the sake of revolution had become a secondary consideration. What mattered was Russia's own security. From "an outpost of Imperialism" Yugoslavia had become a potential ally of the Soviet Union, and the Party must do nothing to imperil its security or integrity.

These abrupt changes of line could have unsettled a more stable body than the Yugoslav Communist Party. Soon fresh dissensions broke out in the Party's Vienna-based Central Committee, giving rise in Moscow to the saying: "Two Yugoslavs, three factions." In due course the members of the Yugoslav Politburo were summoned to Moscow and the leadership of the Party again, "completely renovated" though the red-haired Milan Gorkić somehow survived as Secretary General, with, however, Josip Broz now in the key post of Orgsec or Organizing Secretary.

From the first there was a sharp divergence of opinion between the two, Broz maintaining that the right place for the Central Committee was in Yugoslavia, while Gorkić preferred the relative safety of Vienna. In the end a compromise was arrived at. Some of the Central Committee, led by Broz, would go back to Yugoslavia, while others would stay abroad with Gorkić, who would, however, retain the right to veto any decisions taken by the Party in Yugoslavia. Later, in 1936, Gorkić moved his headquarters from Vienna to Paris, while Broz returned early in 1937 to Yugoslavia, going first to Zagreb.

In Yugoslavia the police were as active as ever and there had been widespread arrests. From Zagreb Broz sent a message to what remained of the Party in Belgrade, asking for "a responsible comrade" from the capital to report to him there. The comrade in question was a tall, good-looking young Montenegrin with a shock of dark hair called Milovan Djilas, who had recently come out of prison. For conspiratorial reasons, neither knew the other's real name. Broz was impressed by the young Montenegrin's enthusiasm and by his clear account of the Party's trials and tribulations, while Djilas was struck

hair-breadth escapes from the police of half a dozen countries; false names; false papers. The existence, in short, of a professional revolutionary.

In the summer of 1937, while still in Yugoslavia, Josip Broz received a message from Paris to say that Milan Gorkić had suddenly been summoned to Moscow. Later came a letter from Wilhelm Pieck, head of the Balkan Secretariat of the Comintern, announcing that Gorkić had been dismissed and instructing Broz to take temporary charge of the Central Committee. After a visit to Paris to settle that body's dislocated affairs, Broz went back to Yugoslavia. On returning to Paris in the summer of 1938 he received another message, summoning him in his turn to Moscow.

Moscow in 1938 was a dangerous place. The great purge was still raging. "I never knew," Broz said many years later, "whether I should come back alive." But he went and went gladly. A crisis had been reached in the affairs of the Yugoslav Communist Party; he must save what he could from the wreck.

On reaching Moscow, he found his forebodings justified. Gorkić and most of the other Yugoslavs had been arrested. The Comintern were now thinking of abolishing the Yugoslav Party altogether. Meanwhile, said Dimitrov, they would like him to take over the post of Secretary General.

Broz was at his best in a crisis and this, he said long after, was the worst crisis he had to face. He told Dimitrov that he accepted the appointment and would make it his business to clear up the mess. "Go ahead," said Dimitrov.

Josip Broz formally assumed charge of the Yugoslav Communist Party in January 1939. War was certain and war, "the locomotive of history," as Trotski had called it, would bring fresh opportunities for revolutionary action. The Party must be ready to take full advantage of them. His first move was characteristic. Returning to Yugoslavia in March 1939, he took the Party headquarters with him. It is easy to imagine the delight of the rank and file. For the first time for ten years their leaders were with them, directing their activities and sharing their dangers.

Broz was determined to put an end to fractional disputes by

by the older man's practical but at the same time human approach to their problems. They discussed the need for an effective youth organization and agreed that Djilas should return as soon as possible with a suitable student from Belgrade University to take over its leadership.

Back in Belgrade, Djilas talked things over with Aleksandar or "Marko" Ranković, a Serbian peasant's son, sturdy and resolute-looking, who had just served six years in jail for his activities as Secretary of the Serbian Young Communists' League. Together he and Djilas picked as head of the Youth Organization a young law student called Ivo Ribar. Dark, dynamic, and totally dedicated, he was the son of a well-known Liberal politician.

In addition to his other duties Broz had been entrusted by the Comintern with the task of despatching Yugoslav volunteers to Spain, where civil war had broken out in the summer of 1936. Broz's life at this time was one long game of hide and seek with the authorities: up and down the length and breadth of Yugoslavia; back and forth across the frontier;

Below: *A group of Yugoslav volunteers during the Spanish Civil War. Josip Broz was involved in providing secret transport to Spain for volunteers. In the course of this work he spent much time in Paris and traveling around Europe with false papers.*

Below: *A Canadian passport, in the name of Spiridon Mekas, and a Swedish passport in the name of John Karlsson.*

Right: *An identity card Broz used to present himself as I. Kostanjšek, qualified engineer.*

giving the Party strong, united leadership. Of the old Central Committee he only retained Streten Žujović, a tall, dark Serb of about forty known in the Party as Crni or Black. In the main he picked younger men with experience of active revolutionary work: Kardelj, Djilas, Ranković, Kidrič, Ribar, and others. Still in their twenties, they had mostly suffered for their beliefs and were known to him for their devotion to the Communist cause. They, for their part, regarded him with affection and respect. *"Stari"* they called him—"The Old Man." His was forty-six.

Making his headquarters at Zagreb, Broz lived under a variety of assumed names, Kostanjšek, Tomanek, Babić. Never for a moment did his neighbors (or the police) suspect that he was anything but what he claimed to be, a prosperous engineer. Always well dressed, with natural good manners and a distinguished appearance, it was easy for him to pass as a member of the bourgeoisie. On his right finger he wore a fine diamond ring bought with the rubles he had earned by translating Stalin's *Short History of the Communist Party* into Serbo-Croat. In the Party he was now known by the conspir-

atorial name of "Tito." Soon it became a rallying cry, a call to revolt.

To the tasks of recruiting, organizing, and indoctrinating Party members Tito brought a lighter touch than his predecessors and a deeper understanding of human nature. He possessed, too, in a high degree that energy of feeling, that personal quality of conviction, which mark the true leader of men. In less than three years the membership of the Party increased from four to twelve thousand.

Recruits came from all walks of life. Peasants, artisans, and poor students plotted and schemed in company with the sons and daughters of cabinet ministers, generals, and rich merchants. Most joined the Party because of the poverty, social injustice, and corruption they saw around them, and also from a dislike of the Pan-Serb hegemony in Belgrade. In a bewildering world, Communism seemed to them the only system that made sense, offering a new loyalty, a new morality, a new set of values, a revealed theology, a body of dogma to solve all their problems. Under Tito's overall direction, propaganda was intensified. In particular everything was done to make Russia and the Russians more popular in Yugoslavia. "It was," he wrote afterward, "our principal activity."

1939: THE GREAT SHOCK

In the summer of 1939 Tito was again summoned to Moscow. At Comintern headquarters the Yugoslavs were still shunned and at the Hotel Lux no one would share their table. "Don't worry," said Tito cheerfully. "One day they'll be falling over each other to sit next to us."

Meanwhile war was coming closer. The talks which opened between the British and Soviet Governments in the summer of 1939 were doomed from the outset. For some months already the Russians had been secretly negotiating with the Germans. On 23 August Ribbentrop arrived in Moscow to sign a Soviet-German Non-Aggression Pact. At the ensuing banquet Stalin drank Hitler's health. On 1 September the Germans, having secured their rear, marched into Poland.

The Soviet-German Pact did not worry Tito. "We accepted it," he said later, "like disciplined Communists, considering it necessary for the Soviet Union, at that time the only Social-

The signature of the Soviet-German Pact on 23 August 1939 came as a shock to all but the most dedicated Communists. It made war inevitable.
Left: Von Ribbentrop, Hitler's foreign minister, signs the German-Soviet Non-aggression Pact. Stalin smiles in the background.
Far left: Hitler announces the invasion of Poland to the Reichstag on 1 September 1939, while German tanks were already rolling over the Polish plains toward Warsaw (below). The Second World War was under way.

After a year and a half of war, Hitler dominated the greater part of Europe. He was able to summon kings and presidents to him in order to inform them of his wishes. Prince Paul visited Hitler at Berchtesgaden (right) and was "invited" to join the German-Italy-Japan Axis.

Below: The important Fifth Party Congress took place in secret in a house in Zagreb.

ist State in the World." After spending four months in Moscow, mastering the latest intricacies of Comintern policy, he returned to Yugoslavia in January 1940 by way of Odessa, Istanbul, and Salonika, using a Canadian passport in the name of Spiridon Mekas, "a naturalized British subject of Croat origin."

Among those awaiting his return was Herta, the young Slovene girl who had become his second wife. Some months later a son was born to them, Aleksandar or Miško. But Tito, who

from now onward remained in Yugoslavia, had little time for family life. The reorganization of the Party and its purge of undesirable elements had still to be completed.

A year later, in the late autumn of 1940, the Fifth Party Conference was secretly held in a house on the outskirts of Zagreb and attended by over a hundred delegates from all over Yugoslavia. The theme of the Fifth Conference was neutrality. With the conclusion of the Soviet-German Pact, the era of the Popular Front against Fascism and of limited Soviet cooperation with the western democracies had come to an abrupt end. For Communists the war which had broken out was not a war of Democracy against Fascism but the Second

Imperialist War between rival groups of imperialist powers. Everything must be done to stop Yugoslavia from being dragged into the conflict. This was the theme of Tito's address and of the concluding resolution. At the end of the proceedings Tito was able to send a message to Dimitrov in Moscow proudly announcing that "complete unanimity" had been achieved. The decks had been cleared for whatever an uncertain future might hold in store.

That this would in fact be neutrality seemed unlikely. Germany now dominated continental Europe and German pressure on Yugoslavia was fast becoming unbearable. Since King Alexander's death in 1934 his cousin Prince Paul, "an amiable artistic personage," as Winston Churchill described him, had ruled as regent on behalf of the king's teenage son, Peter. Internally, he had sought without great success to come to terms with the Croats. Externally, Yugoslavia's position had shifted, first gradually, and then less gradually, away from her traditional friendship with France and Great Britain and closer to Germany and Italy. Prince Paul had visited Hitler at Berchtesgaden and Mussolini in Rome. "Prince Paul's attitude," wrote the British prime minister in January 1941, "looks like that of an unfortunate man in a cage with a tiger, hoping not to provoke him, while steadily dinner-time approaches." In February Prince Paul's prime minister and foreign secretary and in March he himself were summoned to Berchtesgaden by Hitler and invited to accede to the Tripartite Pact linking Germany, Italy, and Japan. In the end they agreed and on 25 March Yugoslavia acceded to the pact in Vienna.

Prince Paul and his advisers had, however, counted without the people of Yugoslavia. As soon as the signature of the pact became known, there were violent demonstrations in Belgrade and elsewhere. *"Bolje rat nego pakt,"* the crowds shouted. *"Bolje grob nego rob."* "Better war than the pact. Better death than slavery." In Winston Churchill's words, the Yugoslav people had found its soul. On 27 March young King Peter was declared of age, Prince Paul and his prime minister placed under restraint, and a national Government formed by an Air Force General named Simović.

On learning what had happened, Hitler gave orders for

42

Yugoslavia accepted the invitation on 25 March 1941 (left). The people of Yugoslavia did not agree to membership in the Axis.

Extensive demonstrations took place in Belgrade and other towns (below), under the slogan: "Better war than the pact. Better death than slavery." The coup d'état against Prince Paul followed, and Hitler, infuriated, ordered the annihilation of Yugoslavia.

At five a.m. on the sixth of April, ten days after the pact was signed, German and Italian troops thrust across the Yugoslav borders (right), after waves of German bombers had carried out devastating air raids on Belgrade (below).

Yugoslavia to be destroyed. Ten days later, at 5 A.M. on Palm Sunday 6 April, the first German troops entered Yugoslavia and soon wave after wave of German bombers were systematically obliterating Belgrade. "Operation Punishment" had begun. The campaign was over in a few days. Skoplje fell on 9 April, Zagreb on 10 April, Ljubljana on 11 April, and Belgrade on 12 April. On 16 April King Peter left the country. On 17 April the High Command capitulated.

Yugoslavia, the Führer had decided, must cease to exist. Her place on the map would be taken in future by a large, nominally independent Croatia, closely linked to the Axis, and by a separate and much diminished Serbia under German occupation. Her remaining territories would be distributed piecemeal among her neighbors, Germany and Italy, Hungary, Bulgaria, and Albania.

One beneficiary of the new dispensation was the Ustaša leader, Dr. Ante Pavelić, who, arriving in the baggage train of the invaders, made on 15 April his triumphal entry into Zagreb as *Poglavnik* of the Independent State of Croatia. There he was given a warm welcome by a substantial number of the population. "These," wrote Archbishop Stepinac, the

Roman Catholic archbishop of Zagreb, in a circular letter to his clergy, "are events which fulfill the long dreamed of and desired ideal of our people. Respond readily to my call to join in the noble task of working for the safety and well-being of the Independent State of Croatia." Once installed, Dr. Pavelić lost no time in setting up a singularly unpleasant dictatorship on Nazi or Fascist lines with his faithful Ustaša in the role of praetorian guard. In matters of race the *Poglavnik* went further than Hitler himself. Croatia, he decreed, must be

purged, not only of Jews and Gypsies, but also of Serbs, who amounted to one-third of the population. "We shall kill some of the Serbs," said his newly appointed minister of religion, Dr. Budak. "We shall drive out others and the remainder will be forced to embrace the Roman Catholic faith." Nominally Croatia was a kingdom, but the young Italian Duke of Spoleto, who had been chosen as king, found it more convenient to stay in his native country.

What was left of Serbia was now placed under direct German

The High Command of the Yugoslav Army capitulated on 17 April 1941. Below left to right: *The capitulation negotiations. Hitler subsequently made a triumphant entry into Zagreb while Yugoslav soldiers were led off to prisoner-of-war camps. The Ustaša leader Ante Pavelić profited by the new situation to advance himself from Hitler's lackey to leader of the independent state of Croatia.*

POSEBNO IZDANJE

HRVATSKE NOVINE

GLASILO HRVATSKOG USTAŠKOG POKRETA ZA VELIKU ŽUPU GORA

Broj 25.	SISAK, 22. srpnja 1941.	God. XVII.

Šest komunista streljano u Sisku

SISAK, 22. srpnja. Osudom pokretnog prijekog suda osuđeno je na smrt sedam sisačkih komunista.

Milošću POGLAVNIKA pomilovan je Aleksandar Ladušić, star 19 godina, na 20 godina teške tamnice. Osuda je izvršena nad osuđenima u 7'15 sati.

Pokretni prijeki sud zasijeda dalje.

Ubijeni komunisti u šumi Kapt. Tišina.

Danas prije podne ubijeni su po oružnicima u šumi u Kaptolskoj Tišini komunisti koji se nalaze u bježanju naoružani i to: Ogulinac Ivan iz Žabna i Lasić Ivan iz Odre.

military control, a puppet government of half-hearted Serbian quislings under General Milan Nedić being later formed for administrative purposes. Slovenia was divided between Germany and Italy. The Italians occupied Montenegro, most of Dalmatia, and parts of Croatia. The Bačka went to Hungary, Macedonia to Bulgaria, and the historic plain of Kosovo to the Albanians. By the end of April, Yugoslavia had ceased to exist.

Reviewing the situation a week or two later in his party's May Day Manifesto, Tito blamed "this terrible disaster" on "the criminal policy of the Belgrade rulers, who cared for nothing but their capitalist interests." Thereafter his attitude appears to have been one of vigilance and preparation. According to his own account he and the Party used the two months that followed the invasion "for final preparation for an uprising, for diversions, for gathering arms, and so on." Any doubts they may have had as to the right course for them to follow were, however, soon to be cleared up once and for all by Hitler's invasion of the Soviet Union. On 22 June 1941 the Second Imperialist War became overnight for Communists everywhere the Great Fatherland War, the People's War for Freedom and Democracy. On hearing the news, Tito, who had moved to Belgrade early in May, at once called together the Politburo in order to discuss this "new situation" and the new measures for which it called. After the meeting, a proclamation was issued, reminding the people of Yugoslavia that the struggle of the Soviet Union was their struggle and calling upon them to take arms, under Communist leadership, against the Fascist invaders "who, like mad dogs, are attacking the Soviet Union, our dear socialist fatherland, our hope and beacon." "This," in Tito's words, "was our Party's war cry, its call to arms and to revolt."

That Tito and his comrades were correctly interpreting Moscow's wishes was clear from a secret telegram which reached them that same day from the Comintern, signed by the code name *Djed*, Grandpapa. "It is," signaled Grandpapa, "absolutely essential that you should take all measures to support and alleviate the struggle of the Soviet people. You must start a movement with the slogan of a united national front, indeed of a united international front, to fight the German and Italian Fascist bandits.... Organize partisan detachments without a moment's delay. Start a partisan war in the enemy's rear."

Resistance to the conqueror produced scenes of horror: burning villages, destruction of property, mass executions. Despite this, resistance grew in every part of the country, aroused principally by members of Communist organizations, who were persecuted by the occupying forces as the most dangerous of enemies. Right: Members of the Communist District Committee of Čačak before their execution. Far right: A cemetery for similar victims in Bukori.

PART II

FEARFUL ODDS

Tito lost no time in giving effect to Moscow's directives. Within two or three weeks of Hitler's attack on the Soviet Union and of the Party's call to arms guerrilla bands under Communist command were operating in Serbia and elsewhere, small groups of determined men and women armed with anything they could lay hands on, cudgels, axes, and old sporting guns. For further supplies they depended on what they could capture from the enemy. They were known as Partisans. In their caps they wore as their badge a five-pointed red star. Soon news began to reach Belgrade of ambushed German convoys and of surprise attacks on enemy units and outposts.

The immediate aim of these operations was to harass the enemy, disrupt his communications, and destroy the morale of his troops. But they also had another, long-term motive, the creation of a Communist Yugoslavia. The time, in Tito's words, had come for the Party "to prepare to seize power and to seize it in such a way that the bourgeoisie would never regain it." At the same time as the war of resistance, a revolution was in progress, the Communist revolution to which Tito, for one, had looked forward all his life.

At first Tito directed operations from Belgrade, where he had installed himself in a villa in the fashionable suburb of Dedinje

only a few hundred yards from the official residence of the German commander-in-chief. From his bathroom a concealed door led to a secret hiding place in the roof, where he kept, in case of need, two revolvers and sixteen hand grenades. Also in Belgrade were Djilas, Marko Ranković, Ivo Ribar, Black Žujović. Kardelj had gone to Slovenia to organize resistance there. The Party was now on a war footing. At the end of June it had been decided to appoint Tito military commander of all Partisan Detachments and to form from the members of the Party's Politburo a general headquarters of National Liberation Partisan Detachments.

Outwardly Tito remained that well-dressed and generally respected citizen, engineer Slavko Babić, spending much of his time at the nearby villa of Vladislav Ribnikar, a rich newspaper owner, who was also a Communist sympathizer. There

Posters were used by the occupation forces to offer a reward of 100,000 Reichsmarks for Tito, alive or dead. No claimants were found for this—under the circumstances—gigantic sum of money.

50

he would preside over meetings of his general staff, planning sabotage operations and despatching couriers to detachments in the field, while Vlado Ribnikar and his pretty young wife kept watch for prowling police agents. By means of a secret wireless set, hidden in a house in Zagreb, he maintained regular contact with Moscow.

On 4 July the decision was taken to extend and intensify the revolt and form stronger and more numerous Partisan Detachments, each with its own political commissar. After the meeting Djilas left for his native Montenegro. Tempo Vukmanović, lean, dark, and decisive looking, was sent to Bosnia and Hercegovina. Kardelj was already in Slovenia. Tito himself, Marko Ranković, and Black Žujović were responsible for Serbia.

Soon reports reaching Tito from the field told of operations on an ever increasing scale. Every day petrol and ammunition dumps were blown up, convoys ambushed, trains derailed, enemy outposts raided, and more arms and ammunition captured. Before long large areas were in the hands of the insurgents, particularly in Serbia. "Partisan operations in Serbia," Tito signaled to Moscow on 23 August, "are assuming to an ever greater extent the character of a national uprising. The Germans are only holding the larger towns while the villages and hamlets are in the hands of the Partisans. All headquarters and commanders of Partisan Detachments throughout Yugoslavia are in direct touch with Partisan HQ under Walter."

From Djilas came news of a spectacularly successful rising against the Italians in Montenegro. Some messages were less encouraging. From Bosnia Tempo Vukmanović reported

After the occupation of Yugoslavia, the leadership of the Communist Party, acting on instructions from Moscow, kept a low profile, and occupied themselves with preparations for the uprising that Tito was convinced must come.

The situation changed dramatically with the German Army's attack on Russia on 22 June 1941. On 3 July Stalin gave orders for guerrilla activity behind the German lines. Posters appeared in Yugoslavia, secretly printed (below left).

On 4 July 1941, the Politbureau of the Central Committee of the CPY, headed by Tito, met in the house of Vladislav Ribnikar (below left) at Dedinje, Belgrade. It was decided that a general people's uprising should start, and a proclamation to that effect was issued. Below: A group of Partisans belonging to the company attached to the Supreme Headquarters in September 1940. Below center: A group of Partisans and leaders of the uprising in Montenegro. Bottom: A Partisan company in Dolenjska, Slovenia.

heavy casualties among the leaders and consequent disorganization. In Croatia, as in Slovenia, there was much that was satisfactory, but signs, too, of inadequate organization. "Form strong Partisan Detachments," Tito replied, "and see that they are constantly in action." "Our great need," he signaled to Moscow, "is for arms. Please let us know if you can supply us with arms." But there was no response.

Toward the end of August Tito decided to leave Belgrade and join his troops in the field. Still wearing his smart city suit and in company with some reliable girls and a friendly Orthodox priest with beard and flowing robes to provide cover, he traveled by train as far as Požega in central Serbia and thence by horse cab in the direction of Krupanj, now in Partisan hands. Well before Krupanj they were challenged by the first Partisan outposts. It was four in the morning when Tito reached his headquarters. At once he got down to work, dealing briskly with the outstanding problems which awaited his attention: By early September the Partisans had gained control of a large area of hill country between Šabac and Užice and here, in the little mountain hamlet of Stolice, he now set up his general headquarters.

When the Partisans first entered the field in Serbia in the summer of 1941, they had found another resistance movement already in existence, the Četniks of Colonel Draža Mihajlović, a serving soldier who, after the capitulation of Yugoslav army in April, had made his way with a handful of like-minded companions to the thickly wooded hill country of western Serbia. Establishing his headquarters on the plateau of Ravna Gora in the Šumadija, he had set about recruiting more volunteers and organizing them under local leaders on a largely territorial basis. For the time being he concentrated on building up his organization and discouraged the idea of active operations against the enemy, which would inevitably have provoked reprisals. His object was not to destroy, but to preserve, to keep in being in Serbia something that could serve as a nucleus from which to rebuild the old order that was so dear to him: the Monarchy, the Orthodox Church, the Army, and the Serbian way of life.

Tito's aim was the opposite. He was a revolutionary with no desire to see the old order restored. He had been fighting

On 26 September 1941 Tito held at his headquarters in the little Serbian mountain village of Stolice (below) a meeting of Partisan commanders from all over Yugoslavia.
At Stolice it was decided to set up a separate command in each different region under the overall control of Tito's Supreme Headquarters and to aim wherever possible at establishing "liberated areas."

The contrast between the opposing forces facing each other in Yugoslavia in the summer of 1941 could hardly have been greater.
From small beginnings Tito's Partisans grew by degrees into a force who could hold their own against the embattled might of the Wehrmacht.
Soon by their guerrilla tactics they were containing a score of enemy divisions which could otherwise have been employed against the Allies on other fronts. A great resistance leader, Tito evoked an immediate

against it all his life and hoped to set up a new, revolutionary order in its place. For him this was a People's War, with the whole population in the firing line, enjoying the same chance of a hero's death as the Partisans. If towns and villages were burned, hostages shot, and families made homeless, this would help swell the ranks of the revolutionaries. His task, as he saw it, was to harass the enemy by every means in his power and not to count the cost. In this he was sustained by the indomitable spirit of the Yugoslav people.

The rising which took place in Serbia in the late summer and early autumn of 1941 was due in part to the organized activities of both Partisans and Četniks. It was also a spontaneous national rising. In the battles which followed Četniks and Partisans fought side by side against the common foe. They were astonishingly successful. The Germans were taken by surprise. Ever larger quantities of arms and ammunition fell into the hands of the insurgents. Soon most of Serbia was free, part under Četnik and part under Partisan control.

It was in these circumstances that Tito and Mihajlović met in mid-September in the village of Struganik at the foot of Ravna Gora. Though both were very much on their guard, the regular officer on the one hand and the professional revolutionary on the other, their discussions were friendly enough. With regard to future operations against the Ger-

response from the Yugoslav people who saw their own best qualities reflected in his. "I wish we had a dozen Titos in Germany," said Heinrich Himmler later.

mans, however, Mihajlović would not commit himself, saying the time was not yet ripe, which made Tito think that he probably did not really mean business. In the end agreement was reached on limited cooperation.

On 26 September, Tito held at his headquarters at Stolice a conference of Partisan commanders from all over the country. Some had come on foot or on horseback from relatively nearby, others, Kardelj for example, had traveled for hundreds of miles by train in disguise and with false papers. Their reports showed that, in addition to Serbia, there were now active resistance movements under Communist leadership in Slovenia, Croatia, Bosnia, Hercegovina, and Montenegro, in short that the movement had become nationwide. It was accordingly decided to set up a separate command in each region, under the overall control of Tito's general headquarters, and at the same time to try wherever possible to establish liberated areas under National Liberation Councils, likewise under Communist control, to take the place of local government.

At the end of September Tito moved to Užice, a flourishing little market town in the West Morava Valley dominating the road and rail communications of western Serbia, where he established his headquarters in the local bank, complete with desks and telephones. Under Partisan auspices a local factory produced four hundred rifles a day. A printing press turned out thousands of copies of the Party newspaper, and the local tobacco factory provided the Partisans with their own brand of Red Star cigarettes. A People's Court tried traitors and collaborators and National Liberation Councils were set up everywhere within reach.

Despite occasional clashes, the uneasy alliance between Partisans and Četniks had persisted and on 26 October another meeting took place between Tito and Mihajlović in the village of Brajići. Though various forms of cooperation were discussed, the meeting again broke up without any firm agreement being reached. Holding the views he did, Mihajlović mistrusted the political intentions of the Partisans, while his doubts as to the wisdom of their aggressive tactics were abundantly confirmed by the Germans' massacre of the entire male population of Kragujevac in retaliation for Partisan

activities. Nor had Mihajlović been made any more anxious
to cooperate with the Partisans by the recent arrival at his
headquarters of a first British liaison officer, Captain Hudson,
whose presence implied the support for his movement of both
the Royal Yugoslav and British Governments. Meanwhile in
Great Britain and America the fame of Mihajlović and his
Četniks was spreading far and wide, while no mention was
made of the Partisans. Any prospect of a permanent understanding between the two movements was manifestly remote.
After a number of minor incidents, a major clash between
Partisans and Četniks took place between Užice and Požega
on the night of 1 November. Further clashes ensued. Simultaneously with the war of resistance, a civil war was in
progress, which both sides would henceforth prosecute with
the utmost energy and vindictiveness.

This internecine strife could only help the Germans, who
since the middle of September had been strongly reinforcing
their troops in Serbia, while at the same time retaliating more
savagely than ever against the civilian population. Using
armor, artillery, and aircraft, they now made a determined
attack on the areas held by the insurgents in the West Morava

Valley, blasting their way along the main lines of communication while simultaneously carrying out encircling movements against the Partisans in the hills.

By the end of November Tito's position in Užice had become
untenable. With strong German forces closing in on him
from three sides, he gave orders to evacuate the town and
withdraw southward across the mountains into the Sandžak,
a barren mountainous area on the borders of Serbia and eastern Bosnia.

While Tito withdrew into the Sandžak, leaving no more
than a few scattered detachments behind him in Serbia,
Mihajlović fell back on Ravna Gora. As he had foretold, the
Partisans' aggressive approach had brought down a terrible
retribution on all concerned. But at least it had led to their
withdrawal from Serbia. And here his interests and those of
the Germans coincided. Both were now fighting the same
enemy. For the Četniks, resistance to the Axis forces of occupation had become far less important than the eradication of
their Communist rivals.

With German approval, the puppet prime minister of Serbia,
General Nedić, had raised certain forces with which to fight

Četniks and Ustaša are frequently mentioned in this book. Both were enemies of the Partisans. Apart from this they had little in common.

The Ustaša were terrorists in uniform, used by Pavelić, the overlord of independent Croatia, to support his regime in the manner of the German SS. The Četniks, formed from remnants of the Yugoslav Army, were a resistance organization.

the Communists. By allowing his men to cooperate with these, Mihajlović could gain a welcome respite, badly needed arms and supplies, and the opportunity of fighting the Partisans under more favorable conditions. He was now on a slippery slope. Liaison with Nedić led, as it was bound to, to liaison with the Germans, while some of his commanders went even further and concluded formal agreements with the enemy. What had begun as "parallel action" developed into collaboration. Nor did the Germans make too many difficulties. "Why," in the words of one of Mihajlović's British liaison officers, "should they? The Četniks were, from the German point of view, doing a useful job of work."

The leader of the Četniks, Colonel Mihajlović, had the support of the government in exile in London, and for a considerable time that of the Allies. Tito tried initially to carry out joint actions with him. The political and military objectives of the two men were, however, irreconcilable.

58

Left: *Ustaša recruiting office.*

Right: *Collaboration between Ustaša and occupiers was complete, frequently with the blessing of individual members of the Croat clergy.*
Collaboration on the part of the Četniks with the forces of occupation was long a controversial topic.

Below: *Cheerfully united, from left to right, a Četnik, a Ustaša, unidentified, a German, and a Četnik.*

Left: *Dr. Ante Pavelić, dictator of independent Croatia and notorious for his massacres on arriving in Zagreb after the German entry into the town.*

Right: *Ustaša artillery shelling Partisan positions.*

THE ENEMY'S OFFENSIVES

Between 1941 and the end of the war the Germans launched seven major offensives against Tito's Partisans.

Right: *Partisans marching through snowy countryside at Bukove.*

During the weeks that followed, Tito, constantly harassed by the enemy, succeeded in bringing his main force of nine detachments through the Sandžak into the snow-covered uplands of eastern Bosnia. On 24 December they reached Rogatica, a little Moslem hill town some forty miles east of Sarajevo. It had been a hard march. Food was short. It was bitterly cold. Morale was low. The Germans had overtaken and massacred a large group of Partisan wounded. Meanwhile Tito, undaunted, had announced the formation of a special corps d'élite, the First Proletarian Brigade, who would wear, superimposed on the red star in their caps, a golden hammer and sickle. To command them, he appointed Koča Popović, a Serbian millionaire's son, who had fought in Spain and enjoyed a considerable reputation as an avant-garde poet. Small, dark, and incisive, he had during the past six months already proved himself a brilliant guerrilla leader.

Tito's arrival in Bosnia helped spread the revolt to another part of Yugoslavia. His task was made easier by a variety of circumstances. Though part of the Independent State of

Left: *The first photograph of Tito as military commander, 1941, with Aleksandar Ranković and Dr. Ivo Ribar.*

Ratko Mitrović, political commissar of the Partisan Detachment, addressing the people on the square in the liberated town of Čačak.

Croatia, Bosnia had a population which was predominantly Serb. To Dr. Pavelić this was an anomaly, requiring immediate attention. Beginning in June, the massacres lasted all through the summer. Soon Bosnia was running with blood. Bands of Ustaša roamed the countryside, slaughtering Serbian men, women, and children, desecrating churches, murdering Orthodox priests, torturing, raping, burning, drowning.

But the excesses of the Ustaša had an important consequence. Before the end of the summer the surviving Bosnian Serbs had taken to the hills, determined to sell their lives dearly. There they had been joined by a number of Croats, more and more of whom had also come to detest the new regime and, under

On 21 December Tito had formed from among the troops he had brought with him from Serbia a special shock unit, the First Proletarian Brigade, who wore, superimposed on the red star in their caps, a golden hammer and sickle. To command this brigade, he appointed Koča Popović.

Below: Tito reviews the First Proletarian Brigade.

Tempo Vukmanović, had succeeded in building up in the mountains round Sarajevo an effective network of Partisan Detachments. Such was the promising nucleus of rebellion which Tito found on reaching eastern Bosnia with the First Proletarian Brigade in December 1941.

It was not long, however, before there was a vigorous reaction on the part of the enemy. In mid-January 1942 the Germans and Ustaša, using ski-troops, made an all-out attack on the Partisans in eastern Bosnia, while simultaneously the Italians in Montenegro sought to stop them from breaking out to the south. But Tito, by a skillful maneuver, somehow succeeded in slipping through the enemy lines, crossing the Sarajevo-Višegrad railway, and eventually reaching safety in the mountains to the south of it, where he set up his headquarters

in the little east Bosnian town of Foča on the upper reaches of the River Drina. The Second Enemy Offensive, as the Partisans called it, had failed in its main objective. At Foča, where he was to remain undisturbed for more than three months, Tito strengthened and re-formed his main force. On 1 March a Second Proletarian Brigade was formed, quickly followed by three more.

From the hills above Foča the Partisans could see the snowy peak of Mount Durmitor, thirty miles away to the south in Montenegro. In Montenegro events had taken a no less dramatic course than in Serbia or Bosnia. By nature and tradition the Montenegrins are warriors. On 12 July 1941 the Italians, to whom Montenegro had been allocated under Hitler's share-out, had declared it a puppet principality. Next morning a national uprising of such violence broke out that it all but swept the invaders into the sea. All over Montenegro Italian garrisons were attacked and Italian convoys ambushed. "The capital," wrote Count Ciano, the Italian foreign minister, in his diary, "has been cut off and all the approaches to it are blocked by the insurgents.... If it were not so deeply and bitterly significant, it would be grotesque." In confusion the Italians fell back on the three main towns, Cetinje, Nikšić, and Podgorica. In a week the rest of the country was free.

A leading part in the rising was played by Milovan Djilas, newly arrived from Belgrade, by Peko Dapčević, a young Montenegrin student who, having fought with distinction in Spain, had recently returned to his native country after a couple of years in French and German concentration camps, and by Arso Jovanović, a former regular staff captain, also a Montenegrin. Politically the tone had been set by Moša Pijade, Tito's fellow-prisoner in Lepoglava, attired for the occasion in Montenegrin national dress.

The Partisans' success in Montenegro was of short duration. Their operations lacked coordination, while what Tito called their "harsh, sectarian, and incorrect attitude" soon alienated large sections of the population. After their initial setbacks the Italians quickly brought in strong reinforcements. Village after village was bombed from the air, the main lines of communication cleared, and strong motorized columns sent out into the countryside to kill and to burn. By the end of the

summer much of Montenegro had been reoccupied and the insurgents driven back into the mountains. Meanwhile, as elsewhere, the local Četniks had by the autumn ceased to co-operate with the Partisans or indeed to fight the Italians, with whom they were in due course to conclude an agreement for joint action against the Communists.

Tito's arrival in eastern Bosnia brought badly needed encouragement to the Montenegrin Partisans, who now set about reorganizing themselves. Larger units were formed and a proper chain of command instituted. By the end of the winter much ground had been regained.

The Partisans' great need was still for arms and supplies. All through the winter Tito had continued to keep Moscow informed of the course of operations, constantly renewing his requests for material assistance. "We await your aircraft day and night," he signaled hopefully from Rogatica on 29 December 1941. But no help came. Early in February 1942 a lull in the fighting enabled Partisan headquarters to establish direct radio contact with Moscow. This seemed to offer the opportunity they had been waiting for. In a signal dated 17 February he explained that there was a safe site near Žabljak at the foot of Mount Durmitor where men and supplies could be dropped by parachute. "If you send us enough military equipment," he signaled, "we can mobilize another hundred thousand men." The arrival of Soviet parachutists would, he added, have "enormous moral and political effect."

The Russians promised to see what could be done and every night from 23 February onward a party led by Moša Pijade waited for a drop on a windswept plateau six feet deep in snow. "Be patient," Tito told him three weeks later. "I still count on the visit coming off." Meanwhile from Moscow

came not supplies, but a flood of censorious messages, criticizing the Partisans for being too openly Communist, urging them to change their attitude toward the Četniks, deploring the formation of Proletarian Brigades, and asking why Tito needed to call himself Tito and could not just use his real name.

At the end of March Tito finally gave up hope and recalled Moša and his men from Žabljak. "For the present," he wrote, "you need do no more night duty. I leave you to decide how to explain it to the men." Moša did his best, but the men took it badly. Some even wept. They had spent thirty-seven nights waiting on that snow-swept plateau for Soviet help that never came.

Meanwhile the Italians, with Četnik support, had launched a fresh offensive against the Partisans in Montenegro, while at the same time the Germans and Ustaša intensified their pressure on the main Partisan force in eastern Bosnia. Their offensive, by Partisan reckoning the third, continued until

June and was largely successful. In the end the Montenegrin Partisans were forced back toward Bosnia and Hercegovina and a kind of Četnik-Italian condominium established in Montenegro, the Italians occupying the towns and the Četniks the country and both methodically hunting down and exterminating any Partisan sympathizers they could find. "We must mercilessly destroy these bloodthirsty men as they would destroy us," wrote Mihajlović to one of his local commanders.

Tito, for his part, remained at Foča until early May. Then, as pressure from the north grew greater and the news from Montenegro more disturbing, he moved southward into Montenegro to assume command there himself, taking with him the First and Second Proletarian Brigades. Again he appealed to the Russians for help. "The situation here," he signaled on 24 May, "is critical. Incessant fighting has left our Partisans exhausted. There is no more ammunition. We shall have to withdraw most of our battalions from Montenegro if they are not to be wiped out.... On all sides both soldiers and civilians keep asking why the Soviet Union does not send us aid."

But still there was no response and when after a month's hard fighting it became clear that the Montenegrin Partisans were facing impossible odds, Tito, having successfully eluded the enemy's fresh attempts at encirclement, withdrew them into the highlands of eastern Bosnia and there incorporated them in his main force, now situated in the remote Sutjeska Valley, between the mountain ranges of Maglić and Zelengora.

He now decided on a bold new course of action. Lack of food made it impossible for the Partisans to stay where they were. Their best hope of replenishing their supplies of ammunition was to resume the initiative. And as usual, in the forefront of his mind was the need to "spread the revolt," to carry its message still further afield. Spring had come at last even in the mountains. By the cover they gave, the leaves on the trees favored guerrilla operations. From west and central Bosnia and from Croatia came encouraging reports. With characteristic resilience, he decided to go over to the offensive and, breaking through the enemy encirclement, push northwestward with all the forces at his disposal in an attempt to form a new

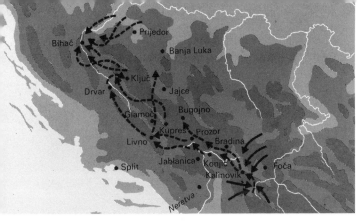

THE GREAT MARCH
June—November 1942

Partisan forces ━ ━ ➤
Enemy forces ━━━➤

In June 1942 Tito began the great march which in five months took his main striking force from Montenegro to the heart of Pavelić's Independent Kingdom of Croatia.

"liberated area" in the very heart of Pavelić's Independent Kingdom of Croatia.

The order to move was given on 22 June 1942. The Partisans' immediate objective was the railway line linking Sarajevo with Mostar and the Adriatic. For the first few days the going was hard. The weather was bad and prolonged lack of food was beginning to tell. Emerging from the woods on the tenth day, Tito with one battalion attacked and took the Ustaša-held village and railway station of Bradina, while other Partisan units struck at other points along the line. In Bradina station they captured a goods train with thirty-three truckloads of food and other badly needed supplies including nearly half a ton of dynamite.

A few days later they took Konjic and after that the little hill town of Prozor. But now they met tougher opposition. Repeated Partisan attacks on the Ustaša strongholds of Bugojno and Kupres were repulsed, while in the Kozara region of central Bosnia a Partisan force and some fifty thou-

sand civilians were surrounded by the enemy and only succeeded in breaking out after several weeks of heavy fighting. On 7 August, however, after a battle lasting more than a week, the Partisans managed to take and hold the town of Livno in western Bosnia and with it most of the surrounding plain.

In barely six weeks Tito, now established at Glamoč in central Bosnia, had moved the bulk of his forces from one part of the country to another and there resumed the offensive. By the end of August most of the hill country of central and western Bosnia was in Partisan hands. Meanwhile, from all over the country couriers brought news of successful Partisan operations and increasing support from the population.

With no outside help, Tito and his main force now continued their victorious progress northward through western Bosnia. By the end of September another score of towns and villages had been taken. Alarmed, the Germans brought up strong reinforcements supported by armor, artillery, and aircraft.

But though individual towns and villages changed hands, the bulk of western Bosnia was now under Partisan control.

For some time a constant source of irritation to the Partisans had been the enemy garrison at Bihać, a town of twelve thousand inhabitants on the borders of Bosnia and Croatia. Its capture on 5 November was the crowning triumph of Tito's long march. Despite the enemy's determined efforts to dislodge him, he was now master of most of Bosnia. In eastern Bosnia his forces had won back the territories they had lost earlier in the year. They had a firm hold on northern and central Bosnia and Bihać gave them a valuable base on the borders of Croatia.

Four months earlier the Partisans had been on the run; they had suffered heavy losses; they had been hungry and exhausted and short of rifles and ammunition. Now, all this had changed. They had covered a distance of some two hundred miles, fighting as they went. With no help from outside, they had captured from the enemy large quantities of arms and ammunition. Everywhere fresh volunteers were flocking to join them. Their detachments had grown into formations. Their numbers were rapidly increasing. From mere guerrilla bands, they had become an army, they claimed, of 150,000 men.

To these changes Tito now gave formal recognition. Since January 1942 the forces under his command had been divided into "Brigades." From them, eight divisions and two corps were now formed, the whole constituting the "National Army of Liberation and Partisan Detachments of Yugoslavia." Tito's new corps and divisions did not bear any very close resemblance, either in size or organization, to the corresponding formations in any ordinary army, the average strength of a Partisan division being about 3,500. But they were better armed than ever before and, in addition to small arms, were now equipped with a certain number of captured anti-tank and other light guns. They possessed a supply system, a system of communications, and a chain of command. And finally they fought, as they had always fought, extraordinarily well.

Simultaneously, the scope of the civil problems confronting Tito necessitated a revision and extension of his political and administrative arrangements. "We shall now," he signaled to Moscow, "set up something like a government, which is to be called the National Liberation Committee of Yugoslavia." The reply he received was not encouraging. "Do not fail," wrote Grandpa, "to give your Committee an all-national Yugoslav and all-party anti-Fascist character. Do not look upon the Committee as a sort of government. Do not put it in opposition to the Yugoslav Government in London. Do not at the present state raise the question of abolition of the monarchy. Do not make any mention of a republic."

Having noted these somewhat negative instructions, Tito went ahead with his preparations for the first meeting of AVNOJ, the Anti-Fascist National Liberation Committee of Yugoslavia, which took place at Bihać on 26 November and was attended by delegates from all over Yugoslavia. One of its purposes was to dispel the impression that the Partisans were bloodthirsty Bolsheviks and show that they were democratic patriots who "took a broad, liberal view of things." On 26 November Tito opened the proceedings. The little hall in which the council met was hung with Bosnian

Smrt fafizmu-sloboda narodu

carpets and decorated with roughly drawn portraits, not only of Stalin, but of Churchill and Roosevelt, and with the flags of the Allies, also home-made for the occasion. They were assembled there, said Tito, to form, not a government, but a political body, political machinery, to help prosecute the fight against the Fascist invader. The resolution passed at the end of the meeting was equally reassuring, guaranteeing "the inviolability of private property" and "individual initiative in industry, trade, and agriculture," stressing that there would be "no radical changes in the social life and activities of the people," and promising free, democratic elections.

The Bihać Assembly was by any standards a stepping stone to victory, an outward and visible manifestation of what, by their own unaided efforts, the Partisans had achieved in less than eighteen months. Tito, one of the delegates noticed, was much moved. At supper that night they drank his health. In replying he came perhaps nearer than usual to revealing what was in his mind, in his heart even. "Whatever I have been able to do," he said, "has been the work of the Party. I was young and ignorant and the Party took me under its wing, and brought me up, and trained me. I owe everything to it."

By the end of 1942 not only the Ustaša, but the Germans and Italians, could scarcely fail to be disturbed at the way in which things were developing in Yugoslavia. From his new capital at Bihać Tito was now effectively controlling large areas of territory nominally under Axis occupation, while by their well-planned and boldly executed operations the Partisans were containing a dozen enemy divisions which could otherwise have been used against the Allies on other fronts. "The Partisans," wrote Dr. Goebbels in his private diary, "have made a football of the Croat Government."

Nor were the successes of the Yugoslav Partisans a matter of merely local concern to the Germans. There was a danger that they might drastically influence the entire course of the war. In North Africa, as on the Russian front, the tide had begun to turn. Italian morale was sagging, and it was clear that before long the Germans would have to reckon with the likelihood of an Allied landing somewhere in southern Europe. With German control so seriously threatened in what Winston Churchill had called the "soft underbelly of Europe," it seemed all too probable that the Balkans might provide the necessary bridgehead for an invasion. Peremptorily summoned to Hitler's headquarters, Dr. Pavelić had found the Führer in a thoroughly fractious mood. The Partisans, he had been told, must be eliminated without further delay. Colonel-General Alexander von Löhr, the German commander-in-chief for southeastern Europe, was then called in and preliminary plans made for an all-out drive against the Partisans early in 1943.

Detailed plans for the campaign, which was to be known to the Germans as Operation *Weiss* and to the Partisans as the Fourth Enemy Offensive, were drawn up at a conference held by General von Löhr in Rome on 3 January 1943. The purpose of the German plan was to encircle and annihilate the Partisan forces in the highlands of Bosnia, now the heartland of the Partisan movement or, as the Germans called it, "Titoland." The German troops earmarked for the first phase of the offensive consisted of four divisions under the command of General Lütters. There were also three Italian divisions under General Gloria and a substantial number of Ustaša and Četnik units under German or Italian command.

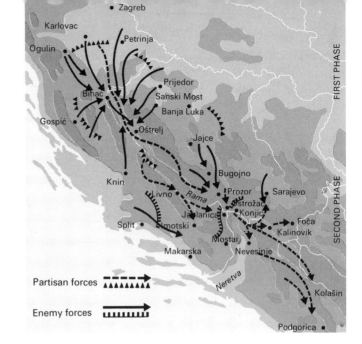

Partisan forces
Enemy forces

FOURTH ENEMY OFFENSIVE
January—March 1943

Below: Tito's order of 3 February 1943 to the First Division telling them not to leave the wounded behind.

Right: The bridge over the Neretva after demolition. Partisans and wounded are shown crossing by the improvised bridge.

The whole force, amounting to some ninety thousand men, was under the overall command of General von Löhr, who flew up from Salonika to see his troops in action.

The Germans and their allies launched their attack on 20 January, its main weight being directed against Partisan positions round Bihać. The Germans attacked from the north and east and the Italians from the south and west, while the Montenegrin Četniks prepared to cut off the Partisan retreat. The attack was supported by vigorous air action against which the Partisans had no real defense.

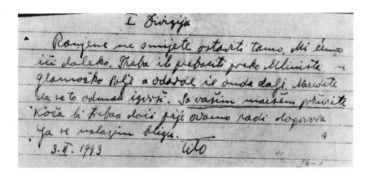

Having received various indications that a fresh offensive was pending, Tito decided to break through where the enemy was weakest, namely in the southeastern sector, held by the Italians and Četniks. Leaving his Seventh Division as a rearguard to bear the main weight of the German attack from the northeast and hold up the enemy's advance for as long as possible, he despatched the First and Third Divisions from central Bosnia on a forced march to the River Neretva in order to forestall the Četnik and Italian forces beginning to assemble along the Neretva Valley and in the key town of Prozor which commanded its approaches. He then ordered his Second Division to move southward through Dalmatia to the Ustaša stronghold of Imotski, halfway between Split and the Neretva, capture it, and then push on to the Neretva Valley. If these objectives could be attained and if, in particular, the towns of Prozor and Konjic could be taken and held, it should be possible for him successfully to withdraw his main force across the Neretva into the wild highlands of eastern Bosnia

and Montenegro and again take the offensive. Meanwhile, with the object of disrupting the enemy's communications and tying down as many of his troops as possible, he gave orders for Partisan units throughout Yugoslavia to launch immediate attacks on enemy garrisons and lines of communication.

Again, Tito's answer to an all-out attack by superior enemy forces was to shift the bulk of his forces as rapidly as possible to another part of the country and there resume the initiative. His task was, however, seriously complicated by having to take with him some three thousand sick and wounded, who, if abandoned, would be massacred by the enemy. For these and for the thousands of civilian refugees who had joined them, the withdrawal was a nightmare. Food was desperately short. Typhus was raging. It was bitterly cold, the country lay under thick snow, and the bright clear weather brought constant air attack.

Ten days after the opening of the offensive, Tito once again appealed to Moscow for help. "Is it really impossible," he signaled, "after twenty months of heroic, almost superhuman fighting, to find some way of helping us?" But the answer when it arrived ten days later simply spoke of "insurmountable technical difficulties," invited them not to lose heart, and sent them best wishes and fraternal greetings. A further signal reproved them for having agreed to a limited exchange of prisoners with the Germans. This was more than Tito could bear. "If you can't understand what a hard time we are having," he signaled back, "and if you can't help us, then at least don't hinder us."

Meanwhile the Partisan main force, taking the sick and the wounded with them and fighting off constant enemy attacks, had covered the best part of a hundred miles and had now

reached the approaches to the Neretva Valley. The River Neretva, toward which they were advancing and which they hoped shortly to cross, is the only river of any consequence to break the mountain range which follows the whole length of the Yugoslav coastline from north to south. Rising in the hills to the south of Sarajevo, it flows for the best part of a hundred miles between steep, craggy, mountainsides to the sea, linking the rugged hinterland of Bosnia and Hercegovina with the smiling Adriatic littoral.

The Partisans' immediate task was to take the Italian-held town of Prozor and so open their way across the Neretva. After two days' heavy fighting, the little hill town fell on 15 February to the Partisan Third Division, who then fought their way through to the Neretva along the valley of its tributary, the Rama, reaching it on 20 February. Simultaneously the Second Division, under Peko Dapčević, having taken Imotski, had reached the Neretva and captured the town of Jablanica from the Italians, while the First Division under Koča Popović had by now also arrived at the Neretva and were besieging a strong enemy garrison at Konjic.

Hitler, who had been closely following the course of Operation *Weiss,* was not best pleased. "It is both impressive and alarming," he wrote to Mussolini, "to observe what progress the insurgents have made with their organization. We are only just in time to suppress the rebellion if we are not to run the risk of being stabbed in the back in case of an Anglo-Saxon landing."

On the last day of February Tito, having established his headquarters in a stone shack in the Rama Valley halfway between Prozor, and the Neretva, sat down with Djilas, Ranković, Žujović, and a few others to discuss their next moves. For the Partisans the situation was perilous in the extreme. The Germans were fast closing in on them from the north and east. One German division was advancing on Prozor, while another hastened to the relief of the beleaguered garrison in Konjic. In Dalmatia the Italians were keeping up the pressure from the west. Beyond the Neretva, on the snowy slopes of Mount Prenj, the Četniks were getting ready to administer the coup de grace to their hated rivals. ("Now is our chance to beat the Communists to their knees," wrote

Mihajlović to one of his commanders. "If we don't take it, it may be the worse for us.")

Having explained the situation to his companions, Tito outlined his plan. It was bold and extremely ingenious. First, he said, the Partisans must destroy all the bridges across the Neretva so as to make the enemy think they no longer intended to break out to the south. They would then attack the Germans to the north of Prozor. This would relieve the pressure on the wounded who were assembled there and at the same time lead the Germans to suppose that this was where they were trying to break out. Then, suddenly changing directions, they would swing back to the Neretva Valley and, improvising a rough bridge, cross the river and break through the Četnik forces on the far side, taking the wounded with them.

As a first step the bridges across the river were blown up. The First and Second Partisan Divisions were then withdrawn from the Neretva and despatched with the Seventh Division to counterattack the Germans advancing on Prozor from the north, while the Third Division held back the Germans advancing from Sarajevo. The attack, directed by Tito himself, went in on the afternoon of 3 March on a twelve-mile front, the Partisans making good use of the tanks and guns they had captured from the Italians. It was a frontal attack against well-trained, well-equipped German troops, possessing the advantages of strong artillery and air support, something the Partisans would normally have avoided, but somehow it succeeded. "Our attack," wrote an eyewitness, "went in like a hurricane. The battle lasted all night. The first two assaults failed, but the third could not be stopped. The Partisans swept down like an avalanche and drove the enemy back to Bugojno."

Against all probability Tito's counterattack had been successful. The enemy had been repulsed with heavy casualties and the Partisan wounded saved, at any rate for the time being. For the moment the Partisans had regained their freedom to maneuver and had also managed to deceive the enemy as to their next move. ("The intention of the enemy," ran a German intelligence report of 5 March, "is to break out to the north.")

By his bold initiative Tito had gained a precious respite. But already strong enemy forces were closing in from all sides on the narrow Rama Valley, where his main force and the wounded were now concentrated. His only hope was somehow to get them across the Neretva before they were all wiped out. For Tito it was a moment of intense anxiety. As he watched the long columns of wounded making their painful way along the narrow valley, an onlooker was struck by the extreme gravity of his expression.

On 5 March, leaving Koča Popović and the First Division to

hold the German advance on Prozor for as long as they could, Tito gave orders for the Second Division under Peko Dapčević to force the Neretva at Jablanica and storm the Četnik positions beyond the river on the slopes of Mount Prenj. They were to be followed by the rest of the main force and the wounded. Meanwhile Third Division would secure their left flank and Seventh Division their right flank.

At Jablanica the Neretva is a turbulent mountain stream about seventy yards wide flowing between steep rocky banks. The point chosen for the crossing was the site of the railway bridge which the Partisans had themselves demolished four days earlier. First it was necessary to establish a bridgehead on the far bank, still held in strength by the Četniks. At midnight on the 6 March a section of Partisans, carrying submachine guns and hand grenades, crawled through the twisted girders of the demolished bridge and, creeping up on the blockhouse, managed to toss a couple of hand grenades into it before the Četniks holding it had realized what was happening. Once they had gained a foothold, they were followed by a stronger force. After some fierce fighting more troops crossed and a bridgehead some five miles in depth was successfully established and held by two Partisan brigades. A rough plank bridge was then threaded through the remains of the old railway bridge. Heartbreakingly all the Partisans' heavy equipment, trucks, tanks, and guns taken from the Italians were jettisoned and sent crashing into the river. And at dawn on 8 March the crossing began.

It was to last for a week. On the first day the sun shone brightly and soon the sky was full of enemy aircraft bombing and machine-gunning. From now onward the weather stayed fine and the Partisans were under constant air attack. But somehow 20,000 men and by now 4,000 wounded, some of whom could not walk, had to be got across one narrow ramshackle bridge, by now under heavy shellfire.

By nightfall on 8 March the whole of the Second Division had crossed and resumed the offensive, extending and consolidating the bridgehead. The movement of the wounded could now begin. Some crawled across on all fours. Others were carried across by Italian prisoners. Every now and then a pony carrying a wounded man would lose its footing and go hurtling into the river with its load. More and more shells were landing everywhere, while from the surrounding hills came the thud of the enemy's artillery and the spasmodic rattle of machine-gun fire. Every day more enemy aircraft filled the dazzlingly clear sky, with nothing more than occasional small-arms fire to keep them off. Already Jablanica was a heap of ruins, its streets strewn with corpses and wreckage. At first light on 11 March Tito and his headquarters staff crossed the river. Prozor had fallen the day before, the enemy were increasing their pressure from every quarter, and the Partisans were now desperately fighting off their attacks on both sides of the river. At dawn on 14 March the last of the wounded were taken across and on the 15th they were followed by the Partisan rearguard.

The Germans were now hard on their heels. Pushing down the Rama Valley, their advanced troops reached the Neretva on 17 March, followed three days later by four more divisions. But the Partisans had eluded them, "leaving," in General von Löhr's words, "neither booty, nor prisoners, nor dead behind them." "The conduct of operations by the Partisan High Command," General Lütters, the German corps commander, was obliged to admit, "was of a very high order and extremely flexible. The fighting qualities of the troops were always good and sometimes exceptional."★

After a month of bitter fighting, the crossing of the Neretva had been accomplished, at a cost of four or five thousand dead. But, though the Partisans had crossed the Neretva, their troubles were by no means over. Their next task was to transport the wounded across the rocky, snow-covered heights of Mount Prenj. Moving slowly in straggling columns, they were exposed to incessant air and artillery attack. Typhus was rampant. Their supplies of food were exhausted; and there was none to be found in the bleak, barren country they were crossing. "Men died where they were sitting," said Tito, "from sheer exhaustion." But somehow the mountain was crossed; they saved the wounded and resumed the offensive.

"And now," in Tito's words, "began the hunting down of the Četniks." Pushing eastward from the Neretva, the Partisans drove what was left of Mihajlović's force of twelve thousand men in confusion before them. "There on the Neretva," wrote Tito, "the Četniks took a beating from which they never recovered." By now things were far from well in the Četnik camp. Mihajlović had little control over his subordinates. Discipline was poor, drunkenness rife. As for the rank and file, their heart was not in it.

"Investigate all cases of desertion," signaled Mihajlović's chief of staff. "Set up a court-martial and execute the ringleaders and all suspects on the spot. Tell the deserters that a hundred have already been caught and that the same fate awaits the others. Their morale must be restored at all costs." But the task was not an easy one. As time went on, more and more Četniks simply went over to the Partisans.

Once the breakthrough was complete, Tito sent his First and Second Divisions on toward the River Drina to open the way to Montenegro and the Sandžak, leaving his Seventh and Ninth Divisions to guard the wounded. By 6 April both the First and Second Divisions had attained their objectives and established bridgeheads on the Drina. Tito now ordered them to continue their advance. Two weeks later they were deep in Montenegro.★

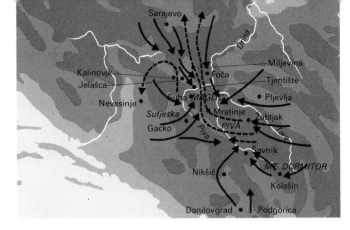

While Tito was advancing into Montenegro, the Germans were preparing to wipe him out. In a sense he had simplified their task. His main striking force, consisting of his First, Second, Third, and Seventh Divisions, was now concentrated in the same mountainous area from which just a year before he had begun his long march to the northwest. There can be few wilder or more inhospitable regions on earth than this great tangle of mountains, forests, and rock-strewn uplands, broken at random by sheer precipices of limestone, falling sharply away to the beds of swirling torrents three or four thousand feet below. In past centuries their mountains had helped the Montenegrins to hold out indefinitely against the Turks. In 1942 the Partisans had themselves been glad enough to fall back into them when hard pressed by the enemy. Now they were to see them in a different light. Their main force was concentrated in an area which was relatively easy for the enemy to encircle but much less easy for them to escape from. By the middle of May the Germans had completed the preparations for their Fifth Offensive, which they called Operation *Schwarz*. To the forces engaged in the Fourth Offensive had now been added the First Alpine Division, the specially trained S.S. Brandenburg Regiment, and various other units bringing their numbers up to 50,000. Three Italian divisions and the elements of others, some Croat formations, and a regiment of Bulgarians brought the total number of enemy troops engaged to well over 100,000 against less than 20,000 Partisans.

The enemy forces were based on half a dozen of the larger towns surrounding the area. The Germans had rightly deduced that it was Tito's intention to strike southeastward. Accordingly the three bases to the south and east of the Partisan positions, Pljevlja, Kolašin, and Nikšić, were held in considerable strength; those to the north and west, Foča, Kalinovik, and Gacko, more lightly.

By 20 May it was evident to the Partisans that their position was becoming extremely dangerous. This time the enemy employed new methods. His aim, as before, was to encircle and pin down the Partisans; to deny them the advantages of mobility and surprise which are a guerrilla's most precious assets and so force them to present a target he could strike at.

But this time the encirclement was better carried out. The Germans employed some of the Partisans' own weapons against them, mobility and surprise in particular. While using the roads to move their mechanized and armored troops rapidly from point to point, they also sent specially trained mobile units ahead of their main force by devious routes to take their opponents unawares. They were quicker, too, to seize points of vantage and dig themselves in and better at preparing ambushes. At the same time the Partisans were kept under continual attack from the air. Finally, realizing how much they depended on the civil population, the Germans forcibly mobilized every civilian they could lay hands on. "Every Partisan found is to be shot," ran one order. "If the local inhabitants are hostile to the German forces, treat them with the utmost brutality. If friendly, harness them in the struggle against the Partisans. Destroy anything that could be of the slightest use to the Partisans. Foul all water supplies."

On 21 May came reports that German units were closing in fast from Foča and Gacko. Next day another German force tried to cross the River Tara and reach the Piva plateau, the triangle of high ground between the Piva and Tara valleys. Tito's position, bottled up on the Piva plateau, completely surrounded, under heavy air attack, with supplies running out and the enemy advancing in strength from all sides, was now hazardous in the extreme. It was clearly essential that he should break out without delay. He could no longer hope to continue his advance to the southeast, now blocked by strong enemy forces based on Pljevlja, Kolašin, and Nikšić. He therefore sent his First Division under Koča Popović on a forced march northward with orders to throw back the Germans advancing from Foča and, acting as spearhead for the main force, to make every effort to break out at that point. On 26 May, however, came the news that the First Division, having, with difficulty, fought their way into Foča, which the enemy were holding in great strength, had found themselves hopelessly outnumbered and had been forced to withdraw. There was, however, another possibility. A week earlier Tito had sent a small force westward across the River Piva to Mount Vučevo to hold a bridgehead there. He now reinforced this position. At the same time he sent a brigade across

The Fifth Offensive was the supreme test for Tito's Partisans. "Never," said Ranković, "have we been in a worse situation." But they survived it nevertheless. The order of German command: "Every Partisan found is to be shot."

Tito, shown here during a lull in the fighting, was as exhausted as his Partisans (below).

the Maglić Massif into the valley of the River Sutjeska to seize and hold the river crossing at Suha. If he could hold these two points, he might succeed in withdrawing his main striking force across the Maglić Massif, cross the Sutjeska, and then continue northward across the Zelengora range toward the Foča-Kalinovik highway. Accordingly, while his Third Division held back the enemy forces attacking from the south, Tito's main force, with the First and Second Divisions leading, began their advance northwestward.

By now, however, a strong German force had managed to establish themselves on the Maglić Massif beyond the Piva, while another attacked the Partisan positions on Mount Vučevo. To cross the Piva and the Maglić had thus become an even more hazardous undertaking, which could only succeed providing the Partisans held the little village of Mratinje, already threatened by the Germans. On 30 May two Partisan battalions managed to reach the ridge above Mratinje just fifteen minutes ahead of the Germans and throw them back from the summit, while the Partisans on Vučevo managed to beat off all enemy attacks. In this way Tito's line of advance was secured and the main force, picking their way three thousand feet down the almost vertical eastern side of the valley, crossed the Piva by a frail rope bridge and, passing through Mratinje, started to climb the no less precipitous western side.

So far, by a miracle, everything had gone according to plan. On 3 June Tito decided that he and the First and Second Divisions would now advance in strength across the Maglić in the hope of breaking through the enemy forces on the River Sutjeska, while the Third and Seventh Divisions, commanded by Djilas, acted as rearguard and escort for the wounded.

Guessing Tito's intentions, the Germans now reinforced their positions on the Sutjeska with another two divisions and soon heavy fighting was in progress in the valley itself. Tito had originally intended to cross the Sutjeska on a wide front, but by 5 June the whole of the far bank was already in German hands, except for a stretch of three miles between Tjentište and Suha, where the Partisans were still, with difficulty, maintaining their bridgehead. At this point the Sutjeska runs through a narrow canyon between the Zelengora range to the north and the Maglić Massif to the south. On both sides almost perpendicular limestone cliffs rise to a height of three or four thousand feet.

On 6 June, on reaching Suha, Tito gave orders for all heavy weapons to be buried. All surplus packhorses were killed and eaten. Next night, while the forward troops held the Suha bridgehead against tremendous odds, part of the wounded were successfully transported across the river. They were followed by Tito and his headquarters staff, leaving the Third and Seventh Divisions to bring up the rear with the remainder of the wounded. On the far side of the river a narrow path led three thousand feet up the rock face to a small plateau, also in Partisan hands.

Having crossed the river, Tito, with his First and Second Divisions, now set out across the heights of Zelengora. Ahead of them the Germans were regrouping and further strengthening their positions, so as to prevent him from breaking out across the Foča-Kalinovik road. From the rear, meanwhile, and from both flanks more enemy forces were rapidly closing in. "Now that the ring is completely closed," ran a German operation order, "the Communists will try to break through. You will ensure that no able-bodied man leaves the ring alive." "Never," said Marko Ranković during one of their rare halts, "have we been in a worse situation."

On the following day, 8 June, the weather cleared. The sun came out and soon the sky was full of Stukas and Dorniers methodically bombing and machine-gunning. Doggedly the Partisans plodded on, day and night, over rough, precipitous country, keeping alive by eating their skinny ponies, and fighting as they went. All round them the mountain echoed with the din of battle. Tito, who had been wounded by a German bomb, marched with his men, his arm in a sling, his face drawn by the stresses and strains of recent months. "In this supreme trial," he signaled to Moscow, "we request your help." But no help came.

Ahead of them meanwhile Koča Popović and First Division were trying desperately to force their way through the German encirclement. Each time they attacked, the enemy counterattacked. Each time they broke through, the enemy rushed fresh reinforcements into the breach. And then on 12 June, when no hope remained, came the news that the First Proletarian Brigade had broken right through to the Foča-Kalinovik road. Other units followed and there was more fierce fighting. But in the end all the enemy's attacks were beaten off and twenty-four hours later the whole force had crossed the road into the deep forest on the other side. "The Germans," said General von Löhr afterward, "were too exhausted to stop them and there were no reserves."

It was not until a week later that the main force was joined by Djilas and what remained of the Third Division, who had suffered heavy casualties in a savage battle against a greatly superior enemy force immediately after crossing the Sutjeska. Sava Kovačević, the divisional commander, a legendary Partisan hero, had been shot through the head as he led his men to the attack. Almost all the wounded they were escorting had fallen into the hands of the enemy and been slaughtered. All in all the Partisans had lost eight thousand killed in the Fifth Offensive alone.

For Tito the lessons of the past months had not been wasted.

He now gave orders that his whole force should first push on together into eastern Bosnia and there divide up, each division going into a different part of the country to spread the revolt. Henceforward, he said, the Partisans would fight the war "on a wide front." Henceforward they would be careful to disperse their forces and not, by concentrating them in one area, present to the enemy a target against which he could strike a single and all too probably decisive blow. On 21 June they crossed the Sarajevo-Višegrad railway. By the end of the month they were deep in eastern Bosnia and had once again resumed the initiative.

On the evening of July 25, 1943, Mr. Winston Churchill, who was spending the weekend at Chequers, received the news of the fall of Signor Mussolini. "This," he said, turning to the present author, who had recently been appointed to command the British military mission to the Yugoslav Partisans, "makes your job more important than ever. You must be got into Yugoslavia at once."

The British Government's decision to recognize the existence of the Partisans had not been easily reached. Since the summer of 1941 King Peter and the Royal Yugoslav Government had been based in London. It was only natural that, in deciding what resistance movement to support in Yugoslavia, the British Government should take their views into account and no less natural that the Royal Yugoslav Government should favor the Royalist Četniks and bitterly oppose the Communist-led Partisans. The result was a widely proclaimed enthusiasm for Milhajlović and what amounted to a conspiracy of silence in regard to Tito.

It was not until the spring of 1943 that the first serious doubts seem to have arisen in the minds of those responsible for British policy as to the reliability of the information at their disposal concerning Yugoslav resistance. The Germans and Italians were of course fully informed on the subject. Both Hitler and Mussolini realized only too well what a serious danger Tito and his Partisans constituted to the Axis, both locally and in relation to the overall strategic position. It was for this reason that, with things going badly for them on other fronts, they had in the first part of 1943 made such a determined effort to wipe him out, without, however, succeeding in their objective.

Not only was some news of enemy troop movements on so large a scale bound in the ordinary course of events to filter through to Allied military intelligence. By this time the British were, by means of Ultra, reading most of the important signals passing between the German high command and their commanders in the different theaters of war including the Mediterranean. It was from these intercepted messages in particular that Mr. Churchill had arrived at the conclusion that a great deal was going on in Yugoslavia about which he was not adequately informed and that the situation there required urgent investigation.

By this time doubts had also occurred to some of these working in the branch of GHQ Middle East responsible for the conduct of Yugoslav affairs. Among these was Captain F. W. Deakin, a young Oxford don, who, on the strength of various items of information coming in from Yugoslavia, including the reports of the British liaison officers with Mihajlović, had come to the conclusion that the achievements of the Četniks had probably been exaggerated and that the military value of the Partisans was at any rate worth investigating. Without much encouragement from his superiors, he persisted and on 19 May 1943 two British liaison officers, Major Jones of the Black Watch of Canada and Captain Hunter of the Royal Scots Fusiliers, were dropped by parachute to the Partisans in Slovenia and Croatia. Some days later Deakin himself and Captain Stewart of the Royal Engineers were dropped into Tito's headquarters, at that time in Montenegro. Deakin arrived to find the enemy's Fifth Offensive at its height and spent the weeks that followed in the mountains of Montenegro, sharing the hazards and hardships of the hard-pressed Partisans. Within a few days of his arrival Stewart was killed and he and Tito wounded by fragments of the same bomb. During this time Deakin had abundant opportunities of judging for himself the fighting qualities of the Partisans. He also received first-hand evidence of the part played by the Četniks. When the situation permitted, he reported his conclusions by wireless to Cairo, where, for one reason or another, his signals do not seem to have received the attention they deserved. An occasional aircraft load of supplies was, it is true, now dropped to the Partisans, but larger quantities continued to go to the Četniks, who were still represented as being the heart and soul of Yugoslav resistance.

Nevertheless, the Allied invasion of Italy made it necessary to pursue every possibility of harassing the enemy on the other side of the Adriatic, while the Prime Minister's personal intervention lent the whole question an urgency which it might otherwise not have possessed. It was thus that in the course of the summer the decision was taken to despatch the present author to Yugoslavia as brigadier commanding the British

military mission to the Partisans and the Prime Minister's Personal Representative. "What we want," wrote Mr. Churchill on 28 July, "is a daring ambassador-leader to these hardy and hunted guerrillas." In his directive the Prime Minister laid particular emphasis on military considerations. Politics should be secondary. Yugoslavia's future form of government must be settled by the Yugoslavs themselves, once the war was over. Shortly before its departure the addition of an American officer, Major Farish, made the mission an Allied one.

Tito, still a shadowy figure as far as the outside world was concerned, was now in his fifty-second year, sturdily built, with iron-gray hair. His regular, clearly defined features were haggard and drawn and deeply burned by the sun, his mouth ruthlessly determined. His light-blue eyes missed nothing. He had the concentrated energy of a tiger ready to spring. As he spoke, his expression changed frequently and rapidly, in turn illumined by a sudden smile, transfigured with anger, or enlivened by a quick look of understanding. His voice was agreeable, but capable of sudden harshness; his dress neat and workmanlike: a plain dark tunic and breeches without badges

of rank; at his belt a pistol in a leather holster; in his cap a small red five-pointed star; on his finger, unexpectedly, a single diamond.

He made no secret of being a Communist; on the contrary, he gloried in it. But, for a Communist, he was unusually ready to discuss any question on its merits and to take a decision there and then, without reference to higher authority. He seemed perfectly sure of himself: a principal, not a subordinate. There were other unexpected things about him: his surprising breadth of outlook; his apparent independence of mind; his never-failing sense of humor; his unashamed

"Delight in the minor pleasures of life": Tito playing chess (right).

Below: *Marshal Tito on the march with his troops, and in discussions with Field Marshal Alexander, after he had obtained recognition from the Allies.*

Liberation, their struggle against the invader, their victories, their sacrifices. Of this they were proudest of all: that they owed nothing to anyone; that they had got so far without help from outside.

That they had achieved much was undeniable. In two years Tito had built up an effective guerrilla force of some 150,000 Partisans, divided into eight corps and twenty-six divisions distributed over Yugoslavia. Each Partisan formation had its own headquarters, linked by wireless or courier to Tito's general headquarters. In the areas they held the Partisans had set up an efficient provisional administration in which the key posts were held by Party members. Already it was clear that Tito and his followers must in the long run become masters of Yugoslavia.

Of the Partisan leaders Tito himself stood head and shoulders above his fellows. He brought to the war of resistance against the Germans the same qualities which had stood him in good stead in the past: leadership, courage, realism, ruthless determination and singleness of purpose, resourcefulness, adaptability, and plain common sense. On the national resistance movement he imposed the same merciless discipline that he had imposed on the Party; he endowed it with the same

delight in the minor pleasures of life; a natural diffidence in human relationships, giving way to a natural friendliness and conviviality; a violent temper, flaring up in sudden rages; an occasional tendency to ostentation and display; a considerateness and a generosity which constantly manifested themselves in a dozen small ways; a surprising readiness to see both sides of a question; and finally, a strong instinctive national pride, which he shared with every one of his followers, from the highest to the lowest. To the Partisans the outside world did not seem of immediate interest or importance. What mattered to them was their Revolution, their War of National

oracle: the Party line. Where there were important decisions to be taken, whether political or military, he took them, took them calmly and collectedly, however precarious the situation. He possessed and could inspire in others an absolute devotion to their common cause, an utter disregard for the dangers and difficulties which beset them. And most important of all, by throwing together Serbs, Croats, Slovenes, and the rest of them in the fight against the common enemy, he had caused them to forget their old internecine feuds and differences and thus achieved within his own ranks a new sense of national unity.

Amid the varying fortunes of war Tito shared the hazards and hardships of his troops under his command. When his Partisans were on the move, he moved with them, covering immense distances on horseback or on foot, through forests or across mountains, in fair weather or foul, with a resilience which would have been remarkable in a much younger man. When there was a lull in the fighting, he would establish his headquarters in whatever accommodation was available: in a hut or a cave or a castle or in a shelter made of branches in the forest. His rule was to make himself and those with him as comfortable as the circumstances allowed. An efficient system of communication kept him continuously in touch with his subordinate commanders throughout Yugoslavia. From wherever he was he exercised effective military and political control. The greater part of his day and night was spent in perusing the signals and reports which came in from all over the country, discussing them with his colleagues, planning future moves, and sending out fresh instructions and directives. He would also regularly inspect neighboring Partisan units and formations and personally investigate the problems of the civilian population. He believed in seeing all he could for himself at first hand. Having dealt with the immediate problems requiring his attention, he would join the members of his headquarters staff in a convivial meal or a game of chess, or simply lie down on the ground and go to sleep. He had the gift, when he chose, of putting his cares aside and relaxing completely. Then he would laugh and joke as if he had not a worry in the world. But at all times of the day and night, whether working or sleeping or eating, he would be ready,

Tito and Moša Pijade

Ivo Ribar

Koča Popović

Tito with a group of commanders in Jajce (Bosnia), 1942

Sava Kovačević

Tito's association with his closest colleagues, comrades in arms, and friends went back in many instances to his five years in prison. This was the case with Moša Pijade (left). There was a small group of revolutionaries who had shared with him the dangers of life outside the law in the period before the war, men like Edvard Kardelj, schoolmaster; Marko Ranković, son of a peasant

Marko Ranković

Edvard Kardelj

Milovan Djilas

farmer; Koča Popović, son of a millionaire; and Peko Dapčeviyć, these two both very successful military commanders. Also of this group were Ivo Ribar, brilliant speaker, and the Montenegrin Milovan Djilas, one of the Party's leading theoreticians. And the number of his comrades grew continually in the forests.

Left: *Ivan Milutinović*

on the receipt of an urgent signal, at the sound of nearby fighting or at the warning cry of a sentry, to spring into immediate and effective action. Alertness and quick reactions had long been part of his stock-in-trade. An emergency served to sharpen and heighten his powers.

Tito's immediate associates had the same background as he did himself. They were the little group of revolutionaries whom he had himself brought together, who had shared his exiles and his imprisonments, who had helped him organize workers' cells and promote strikes, who had run with him the gauntlet of police persecution, who together with him had formed the new leadership of the Party after the purge of 1937, and who under his leadership now formed the high command of the Movement of National Liberation. Edo Kardelj, the schoolmaster from Slovenia, now the Party's leading Marxist dialectician; stocky, pale-skinned, sensible, and immensely reliable, with steel rimmed spectacles and a neat little mustache. Marko Ranković, the peasant's son from Serbia with his air of conspiracy who, under Tito's supervision, now operated with subtlety and ruthlessness the Party machine and its widespread intelligence organization. Djilas, the Montenegrin intellectual, handsome, intolerant, and impetuous, with a look of inspired fanaticism. Ivo Ribar, young, energetic and dedicated, with the wide brow and high cheekbones of the typical Slav, a brilliant speaker. Black Žujović, tall and saturnine, Tito's Deputy Commander-in-Chief, thrown in again and again where there were dangers to be overcome or difficulties to be straightened out. Koča Popović and Peko Dapčević, his two most famous commanders. Nearly all were in their twenties or thirties, an exception being Moša Pijade, who shared with Kardelj and Djilas the distinction of being the Party's leading theoretician.

There were two striking things about this oddly assorted group over whom Tito presided with an air of amused benevolence: first, their devotion to the Old Man, as they still called him; and secondly, the fact that all of them had been with him "in the woods" since the early days of the resistance and had worked underground with him before that, sharing with him hardships and dangers, setbacks and successes. This common experience had overcome differences of race or class or temperament and had forged between them lasting bonds of loyalty and affection. They had, in short, become comrades in the deeper, nonideological, sense of the word.

Early in September the Partisans seized the opportunity presented by the Italian surrender to occupy the areas previously held by the Italians and more important still, to seize the supplies, arms, and equipment of ten Italian divisions. This enabled them to equip thousands more volunteers and represented a significant accession of strength to their cause. To the

Germans, hard pressed on the Eastern Front and in Italy and still afraid of an Allied landing in the Balkans, they had become an even more serious menace. There were now few parts of the country where they were not operating in considerable strength, and the latest German estimate put their total number at some 111,000 fighting troops. To contend with this menace a new command known as Army Group F was established in Belgrade under Field Marshal von Weichs. There were now stronger German forces in Yugoslavia than ever before, amounting by the end of 1943 to fourteen German divisions, two German SS regiments, and five divisions of non-Germans under German command, in other words well over 200,000 men, in addition to another 160,000 Bulgarian and Serb and Croat quisling troops, making over 360,000 men in all.

With these forces the Germans launched in the second half of September their Sixth Offensive, to be known as Operation Kugelblitz or Thunderbolt. In a few weeks they had successfully reoccupied most of the areas evacuated by the Italians, including Slovenia, Dalmatia, and all the Adriatic islands except Vis. They next turned their attention to Bosnia.

On the strength of firsthand experience the British military mission had reached the conclusion that the Partisans were an extremely effective and well-led military force causing serious embarrassment to the enemy and containing upward of a score of enemy divisions. In the light of their reports it was accordingly decided to give the Partisans all possible help, and soon they were receiving air supplies and air support on a much increased scale. At the same time British officers, linked by wireless to the mission's headquarters, were dropped to the principal Partisan headquarters throughout Yugoslavia.

At the end of November, Tito, undeterred by the enemy's Sixth Offensive, called a second meeting of his Anti-Fascist Council. This was held in the little Bosnian hill town of Jajce,

where he now had his headquarters, and was attended once again by delegates from all over Yugoslavia. In his opening speech Tito told them that the time had come to turn their council into a proper constitutional body and also form a National Committee of Liberation with the powers of a provisional government, designed to supersede the monarchy and exiled government. Tito's speech was received with enthusiasm and the necessary resolutions passed unanimously. Before dispersing, the delegates bestowed on Tito the title of Marshal of Yugoslavia together with the posts of prime minister and minister of defense. For the first time since coming out of prison eleven years before he used his real name of Josip Broz.

In one quarter, the council's decisions were received without enthusiasm, namely in Moscow. Meeting in Teheran at the end of November, Churchill, Roosevelt, and Stalin had discussed the Yugoslav question from a purely military point of view and, in the light of the information available, had agreed that material help should be given to the Partisans. The more delicate political question had been conveniently shelved. Now, without prior consultation or authority, Tito had presented them with a *fait accompli*. To Stalin this amounted to gross indiscipline. It also boded ill for the future. "The Boss," said the former Secretary General of the Comintern to the Yugoslav Party's representative in Moscow, "is quite exceptionally angry. He says that it is a stab in the back for the Soviet Union and for the Teheran decisions."

Tito, however, had other worries. The winter was bitterly cold. In December strong German mobile columns, including ski-troops, converged on the Partisans in the hills to the east of Sarajevo. There was much heavy fighting and the Partisans suffered badly from lack of food and clothing. Toward the end of December the main theater of operations shifted to central Bosnia. The Partisans were driven out of Jajce and

Banjaluka and in mid-January Tito was obliged to move his headquarters to Potoci in the wooded hills above Bosanski Petrovac. Here the commander of the British military mission, who, after reporting to the Prime Minister, had been dropped back into Yugoslavia by parachute a few hours earlier, delivered to him a friendly personal letter and signed photograph from Mr. Churchill which he was clearly much pleased to receive. By the end of February the enemy's Sixth Offensive had spent itself and Tito, with his usual resilience, once again went over to the attack, at the same time moving his headquarters down from the hills to a cave overlooking the little Bosnian town of Drvar.

Some weeks later came a fresh sign of recognition for the Partisans, when, with the assistance of the Royal Air Force, a Soviet military mission under the command of Lieutenant General N. V. Korneyev was landed in Bosnia by glider. For one reason or another, however, it was apparently still impossible for the Red Army to give the Partisans the material aid for which they had so long been asking. From Great Britain and America, on the other hand, they were now receiving help on an ever increasing scale.

Having redistributed their military strength, formed a provisional government, and gained a measure of recognition from the Allies, the Partisans, after three years on the move, were beginning to feel the need for a firmer base, for an island of permanently liberated territory from which to conduct operations. After a couple of relatively quiet months at Drvar it seemed to them that this might now be possible.

They were to be sharply disillusioned. On the night of 24 May Tito lay down to rest as usual in his cave. He awoke not many hours later, just as it was getting light, to find that a number of German aircraft were methodically bombing the village of Drvar. Next came six big JU 52's flying in formation down the valley. From these, while others followed, dropped not bombs, but parachute troops. Soon the first of them were shooting their way into the village. Gliders followed with arms and more men. Before long the whole cliff face was under fire and a heavy machine gun was firing directly into the cave. A Partisan who started out on a reconnaissance fell dead at Tito's feet. There was no escape that way, but, with great good luck, Tito and his companions somehow managed to scramble up the channel of a waterfall at the back of the cave and so reach the cliff top above, which Marko Ranković and a few Partisans had managed to keep clear of Germans. Though heavily outnumbered, the Partisans now counterattacked and momentarily drove the enemy back. Then came the news that strong enemy motorized and armored forces were closing in on Drvar from all sides. Realistic as always, Tito gave the order for a general withdrawal into the hills. The strong German forces, whose arrival had been intended

Not even the use of paratroopers enabled the Germans to achieve success with their Seventh Offensive.

to coincide with the airborne attack, did not reach Drvar till next day, by when Tito was in relative safety. Like its predecessors, Operation Rösselsprung, as the Germans called their Seventh Offensive, had failed in its immediate objective.

For the next few days Tito, a few hundred Partisans, and the Allied missions dodged through the woods, moving mostly at night and lying up during the day while British aircraft based in Italy gave all possible air support. There were many narrow escapes. Tito himself directed the operations both of the little force which accompanied him and of the larger Partisan formations in the neighborhood. Those with him were struck by his calm decisiveness. With four divisions under command, it was not long before he had regained the initiative. "I wish," said Heinrich Himmler enviously a few weeks later, "that we had a dozen Titos in Germany, leaders with such determination and such good nerves, that even though they were for ever encircled they would never give in."

Tito's own inclination would have been to stay in Bosnia, but in response to advice from Moscow, relayed by General Korneyev, he now asked the British mission, who were in constant wireless communication with the Royal Air Force in Italy, to try to arrange for the headquarters party and the missions to be evacuated by air. With some difficulty, this was done, and an hour or two after taking off from a hastily improvised landing strip under the noses of the enemy, he was coming in to land at a British airfield in Italy.

An important stage on the route to Tito's Yugoslavia
was his meeting with Winston Churchill in Naples on
12 August. The meeting was at Churchill's request and
constituted for Tito the first and most important sign of
recognition by the Allies.

It would have been unlike Tito to stay in Italy as a refugee.
A few days later he was landed by a British destroyer on the
island of Vis, where some months earlier the Partisan garrison
had been reinforced by a British commando brigade. Here he
set up his headquarters in a cave high on the slopes of Mount
Hum, whence he at once reestablished wireless communication with his commanders on the mainland. Already the
Seventh Offensive had spent itself and the initiative passed
once again to the Partisans, now receiving massive support
from the Western Allies.

The British had by this time finally resolved the problem of
their relations with the Četniks. Some months earlier Mr.
Churchill had decided to give Mihajlović a last chance,

*After the meeting with Churchill
the island of Vis in the Adriatic
became Tito's headquarters. It was
in a cave on the island that he met
the politbureau in June 1944
(below right). Also on Vis, Tito
reencountered his first son Zarko
(below far right).*

informing him that, unless the Četniks had within a reason-
able time destroyed a certain bridge on the Belgrade-Salonika
railway, all British liaison officers would be withdrawn and
all supplies cease. The appointed period elapsed. The bridge
was not destroyed. And in May all British officers serving
with the Četniks were withdrawn. In Serbia all Allied help
now went to the Partisans, bringing them considerable psy-
chological and political, as well as purely military advantages.
"The reason why we have ceased to supply Mihajlović with
arms and support," Mr. Churchill told the House of Com-
mons, "is a simple one. He has not been fighting the enemy
and moreover some of his subordinates have been making
accommodations with the enemy."

For the Western Allies another, no less difficult problem now
remained to be resolved: How to reconcile their *de jure* obliga-
tions to the Royal Yugoslav Government-in-Exile with the
de facto situation in Yugoslavia and their military alliance
with Tito. Consultations began; pressure was brought to bear;
and in May King Peter on British advice invited Dr. Ivan
Šubašić, at one time Ban or governor of Croatia, to form a
new government for the avowed purpose of coming to terms
with Tito. Early in June, Tito, anxious to secure Allied recognition for his regime, grudgingly agreed to receive Dr. Šubašić
on Vis and on 16 June a provisional agreement was concluded
between the National Committee and the Royal Government under which the Royal Government promised in
future to support the Partisans and both parties agreed that
the question of the monarchy should be decided by the
Yugoslav people after the war. Nominally Mihajlović had
held the post of minister of war in the Royal Government.
He was now abruptly dismissed and King Peter in a broadcast

called on the people of Yugoslavia to transfer their support to Tito. For Mihajlović, to whom the monarchy had meant so much, this final repudiation must have been a bitter blow. Tito's presence on Vis offered a convenient opportunity for discussions with the Allied high command. Early in August he flew to Caserta for talks with General Wilson, the supreme Allied commander, Mediterranean, who received him with every mark of respect. The talks went well and some days later Tito was about to return to Vis when he was told that Mr. Winston Churchill had arrived in Italy and wanted to meet him.

The two met on 12 August on the terrace of a villa overlooking the Bay of Naples, Tito in his new Marshal's uniform, Churchill in white ducks and an open-necked shirt. Their talks ranged over a wide field and were cordial in tone. Churchill told Tito of his admiration for the Partisans and of his determination to afford them all possible help. They also discussed the probable future course of the war in the Mediterranean and elsewhere. On the political side Mr. Churchill made it clear that he recognized the preponderant part Tito and his followers were bound to play in postwar Yugoslavia and explained why the British Government could not formally recognize his National Committee until they had reached agreement with the Royal Government-in-Exile. He also counseled moderation in dealing with the Serbian peasantry and recalled that Stalin had told him that his fight to collectivize Soviet agriculture had been tougher than any wartime battle. Tito replied with studied restraint. What the Yugoslavs learned from the Russians, he said, would be adapted to their own special circumstances and needs. Only when the Četniks were mentioned did his voice take on a more incisive tone. There were three meetings, a dinner, and a luncheon. The ice was soon broken. Before long the two were on friendly terms, as they exchanged jokes and reminiscences. "What struck you most about Churchill?" this author asked Tito on the way back to Vis. "He is a very human man," he replied with revealing perceptiveness.

Tito could be well satisfied with his visit. Apart from the assurances he had been given of continued Allied assistance, the manner of his reception clearly marked the degree of recognition he had now won from the Western Allies. And

In July 1943 the author of this book, then Brigadier Fitzroy Maclean, was appointed head of the British military mission to Tito's headquarters. All British liaison officers reported to him, and he reported directly to Churchill. In September he was dropped by parachute to Tito.

Below: *Tito and Brigadier Maclean.*

now due recognition seemed about to come from another quarter, from the quarter which to Tito mattered most of all, from the Country of the Revolution. By the end of August the Red Army had entered Roumania and was rapidly approaching the borders of Yugoslavia. Early in September Tito put forward through the Soviet military mission the suggestion that he should visit Moscow for the purpose of coordinating his operations with those of the Red Army during the next phase of the campaign. His suggestion was accepted and on 21 September he left the island of Vis secretly in a Soviet aircraft, flying first to Roumania to the headquarters of Marshal F. I. Tolbukhin, the Soviet supreme commander, and then to Moscow.

Four eventful years had gone by since Tito's last visit to Moscow. Then he had gone there as a Comintern agent, the representative of a not very important illegal Balkan Communist Party. Now he returned as the liberator of his own country, a Marshal in his own right, and the leader of a Party shortly to assume power. Gone were the days when he was shunned by his fellow-diners at the Hotel Lux. This time a magnificent *dacha* was placed at his disposal and no sooner

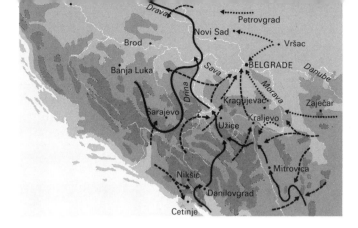

THE LIBERATION OF BELGRADE
Autumn 1944

Partisan forces ◾◾◾▶ Enemy forces ━━▶
Soviet forces ••••••▶ Enemy defensive line ▬▬▬

Below: *Tito visited Moscow in September 1944 to discuss with Stalin the terms on which the Red Army would operate on Yugoslav soil.*
Tito and Stalin during their discussions.

had he arrived than he was swept off to the Kremlin to see Stalin, who embraced him with such enthusiasm that he lifted him clean off his feet.

As the meeting progressed, however, things went less well. Tito, it must be admitted, was not being altogether easy. Stalin had assumed that, when the Red Army entered Yugoslavia, the Partisans and anyone else who might be there would automatically come under the command of Marshal Tolbukhin. Nor had it occurred to him that he might have

to ask anyone's permission before letting his troops cross the Yugoslav frontier in pursuit of the enemy. But he did not know Tito. The latter had come in the name of his National Committee (formed against Stalin's express instructions) to negotiate an agreement which, on certain specified conditions, would permit Soviet troops to enter Yugoslavia for a limited period for the specific purpose of conducting operations against the German forces in Hungary, on the clear understanding that they withdrew again as soon as their task was completed. He was also prepared to discuss joint operations by Partisan and Soviet forces and would be glad to accept the support of one Soviet armored division in the forthcoming assault on Belgrade. There could, he stressed, be

no question of the Partisans being placed under anyone's command except his own, or of the Russians exercising any civil or administrative powers while on Yugoslav territory. Stalin accepted these terms. This was not the moment for a showdown. That could come later. Instead, however, of the armored division for which Tito had asked, he announced that he would send a corps, as a reminder, perhaps, that armed force on a sufficient scale did count for something.

Turning to politics, Stalin, like Churchill before him, counseled moderation, but without great success. "Be careful, Walter," he said. "The bourgeoisie in Serbia is very strong." "I disagree with you, Comrade Stalin," replied Tito. "The bourgeoisie in Serbia is very weak." Stalin then mentioned the names of several non-Communist politicians with whom it might be possible to work, but whom Tito at once dismissed as "scoundrels and traitors." "To you, Walter, they are all scoundrels," said Stalin. "Exactly, Comrade Stalin," replied Tito. "Anyone who betrays his country is a traitor." "From now onward," Tito tells us, "the talks proceeded in a very painful atmosphere." In the end Stalin carried Tito off to supper at his *dacha* in the country, where he plied his guest with so much wine and vodka that he felt ill. The visit had not been an unqualified success, though Tito had certainly held his own. From Moscow Tito flew directly to Vršac in the Banat in time to see his Partisans join up with the Russians as they came flooding across the Roumanian border.

In August Tito had moved nine divisions, grouped in two corps under the overall command of Peko Dapčević, from eastern Bosnia and Montenegro into western Serbia, whence, after a number of sharp encounters with Germans, Bulgarians, and Četniks, they had pushed northward toward Belgrade. At the same time a force which had been moved to Serbia earlier under Koča Popović was brought up to seven divisions, likewise grouped in two corps. As the Red Army advanced toward the Danube, the stage was set for the liberation of Belgrade.

If the Germans were to stop their flank being turned and their retreat cut off, their best hope was to fall back from Greece and Yugoslavia to a defense line further north. This task was entrusted by Hitler to General von Löhr, who began his withdrawal at the beginning of September. Immediately the Partisans, in concert with the RAF and United States Air Force, launched a series of determined attacks against enemy lines of communications throughout Yugoslavia, the German position being further aggravated by the defection of the Bulgarians, who chose this moment to change sides. By the end of September Koča Popović's forces were in possession of most of southern and eastern Serbia, while Peko Dapčević's First Army, advancing northward through western Serbia, were only twenty miles south of Belgrade.

While one strong Soviet force closed in on the capital from the northeast, another converged on it from the southeast, linking up with Dapčević as he advanced from the south. In a desperate attempt to secure their communications with the south until they had withdrawn all their forces from Serbia and Macedonia, the Germans now reinforced the Belgrade garrison with every soldier they could find. The ensuing battle for the city was a singularly savage one. Soon the approaches to Belgrade and the country round it were littered with burnt-out tanks. But by 14 October Dapčević had, with Soviet support, broken through the enemy's front to the south of Belgrade. Led by the First Proletarian Division, the Partisans now launched their assault on the center of the city. It was to last for almost a week, the Germans stubbornly defending every street and every house, but in the end their resistance began to weaken. Early on 20 October the First Proletarian Division stormed and took the Kalemegdan, the old Turkish citadel above the river, and a few hours later the enemy were falling back headlong across the Sava to Zemun, having lost 16,000 dead and 8,000 captured in the battle.

A few days after the fall of Belgarde Tito held a review of his troops, led by the First Proletarian Brigade. The Partisans who marched past him were a variegated throng. Their arms, equipment, and uniforms had mostly been captured from the enemy in battle. But they marched well and held themselves proudly. For three years they had fought up and down the length and breadth of Yugoslavia, enduring innumerable hazards and privations. Now they were entering the capital as conquerors. After they had marched past, Tito spoke to them. He was clearly much moved. "In the most difficult hours of the war," he said, "during the most terrible offensives, I always thought to myself, 'In Belgrade we began the uprising, in Belgrade we shall end it in victory!' That great day has now come. Among us there are very few of those who set out in 1941. They built their lives into the foundations of this country so that it might be free and what the people wished it to be. Their example was followed by thousands of others. Every rifle that fell to the ground was seized by ten other hands. Glory to the fighters who fell for the liberation of Yugoslavia, for the liberation of her capital, Belgrade!"

The victorious Partisans enter Belgrade, October 1944. Partisan units and strong Russian formations had previously, on 14 October, broken through the enemy positions. On the 20th the first Proletarian Brigade stormed the old Turkish Citadel of Belgrade. A few hours later the city was free of the enemy.

From Belgrade the Germans continued their withdrawal as best they could. Within a few weeks Serbia, Macedonia, Montenegro, Dalmatia, and most of Bosnia were free. To safeguard their withdrawal northwestward, they still clung to the main Sarajevo–Brod–Zagreb line of communication. Their northeastern flank, threatened by the Russians in Hungary, they protected by holding on to the Srem, a wedge of territory bounded by the Sava, the Drava, and the Danube, where they formed a fixed front. This they somehow held throughout the winter.

Tito now controlled most of Yugoslavia. His troops occupied all the areas which the Germans had evacuated. His civil authorities had taken over the administration with Party members in key positions. In Belgrade his National Committee ruled as a government. Nor had he any serious rivals. General Nedić had fled from Belgrade in September, handing over the command of his forces to Mihajlović. Many Četniks had by now joined the Partisans; others were fleeing northward with the Germans. Dr. Pavelić still lingered in Zagreb, but his independent kingdom of Croatia was in ruins.

As he resumed negotiations with Dr. Šubašić, Tito had all the cards in his hand. Soon a draft agreement was drawn up, under which Tito's Anti-Fascist Council remained the supreme legislative body, while a combined government was formed from members of the National Committee and the Royal Government. After the war, free and fair elections, it was repeated, would decide the future form of government. Meanwhile King Peter would be represented in Yugoslavia by a Regency. The agreement was submitted to both the British and Soviet Governments and approved by both. After witholding his consent for as long as he could, King Peter gave his agreement in March. From the first Tito had made it clear that his only object in accepting a compromise of this kind was to obtain Allied recognition. Once the Regents had been sworn in and a combined government formed with Tito as prime minister and Dr. Šubašić as foreign secretary, a British ambassador was appointed to Belgrade, where he was joined not long after by Soviet and American colleagues. As Tito remarked with a grin, it had all been "as good as a play."

The war in Europe was almost over. Early in April the Partisans launched a final offensive which was to last until May and in which all their available forces were engaged. Attacked from every side, what remained of the German army of occupation fought their way out through Croatia and Slovenia as best they could. During the last two months of the war, they had lost close on 100,000 killed and over 200,000 captured. Before the main force could reach the frontier with Italy or Austria and surrender to the British, they received on the night of 7 May the order for immediate, unconditional surrender. They could now only surrender to the Partisans. General von Löhr chose to remain in Yugoslavia with his troops. As they were setting out to arrange the surrender, his chief of staff asked him what treatment he himself expected from the Partisans. *"Mit Sicherheit,"* he replied, *"den Tod."* "Death for a certainty." He was not mistaken.

With the retreating Germans went a number of Tito's domestic opponents, Ustaša, Četniks, Serb Volunteer Corps, and others, united in this final act of collaboration with a defeated enemy. Large numbers of them, having failed to escape or having been handed over by the Allied forces, were rounded up by the Partisans and put to death as traitors. It was the predictable end of a war fought as this one had been fought.

Of their leaders one was luckier. "If we must die," declared Dr. Pavelić to a gathering of Ustaša women on 4 May, four days before the fall of Zagreb, "let us die as heroes." After which, outdistancing his own panic-stricken forces, he left headlong for the Austrian frontier, to find asylum eventually in South America. Another decided differently. Declining a British offer of asylum, Draža Mihajlović, at the head of a few faithful followers, made his way back to Bosnia, determined to carry on his fight against Communism to the bitter end. The Germans, the Ustaša, and the Četniks were smashed. For the Partisans the war was now over, leaving them alone in the field and masters of their destiny.

The day when all the regions of our country will be free is not far away. Victory is very near. But let us not be too carried away by our successes in the battlefield, but rather think of how we are going to build our towns, our railways, our roads, our villages and fields, so that the coming generations will be able to say that their fathers did everything they could to leave them a better inheritance....

Tito, 27 March 1945

PART III

DECLARATION OF INDEPENDENCE

Meeting in Moscow in October 1944, Churchill and Stalin had agreed that after the war British and Soviet influence in Yugoslavia should be on a fifty-fifty basis. But already there seemed little doubt that the Soviet share would be greater. Long before the end of the war large numbers of Soviet military and other advisers had made their appearance, in Belgrade; and in April 1945, as though to set the seal on their special relationship, Tito had gone to Moscow to sign a Treaty of Friendship and Mutual Assistance.

Meanwhile relations between Yugoslavia and the Western Allies had deteriorated sharply. One of Tito's war aims had been to annex Trieste. The Allies insisted that the question must be decided at the Peace Conference. By the beginning of May strong British and Yugoslav forces were confronting each other in the city itself. After a number of angry exchanges, Tito, faced with the choice of either withdrawing or risking hostilities with a greatly superior adversary, let it be known that he was prepared to negotiate and on 9 June provisional agreement was reached. An armed clash had been avoided, but the Yugoslavs were seething with resentment. Worse still, Tito's Soviet allies had on this occasion also left him in the lurch—a betrayal which brought from him an angry outburst at the end of May. "We do not," he said, "want to get involved in any policy of spheres of influence.... Never again will we be dependent on anyone." A week later came a sharp official protest from Moscow.

There had been other differences with Moscow before this, trouble over the behavior of the Red Army in Yugoslavia, trouble over a comparison drawn by Djilas between Soviet and British officers, trouble over attempts by the Russians to induce Yugoslav citizens to spy for them. But these minor causes of irritation paled into insignificance when compared with the massive hostility building up between Yugoslavia and the Western powers, from whom, now that he had gained their official recognition, Tito had nothing more to expect.

As was to be foreseen, Tito had lost no time in pressing on with what had long been his chief purpose in life, namely the establishment of a Communist regime in Yugoslavia. Dr. Šubašić and his former colleagues played no part in the new government. Soon after its formation they resigned and were placed under house arrest. By the autumn of 1945 Tito felt ready to hold elections to a constituent assembly. There was a single list. Of the 510 candidates nominated 470 were Communists, while the remainder were Communist-sponsored. Not surprisingly, all were elected by a large majority. Once elected, the Constituent Assembly abolished the monarchy and replaced it by a Soviet-style federative republic composed of six federal republics, Serbia, Croatia, Slovenia, Bosnia, Macedonia, and Montenegro. Both in the republics and at the center the Party was all powerful, providing not only the motive power, but the framework which held the whole structure together. Meanwhile the courts dispensed Communist justice and a vigilant and ubiquitous security police dealt summarily with any possible enemies of the regime. Of these the most prominent was Draža Mihajlović, who for ten months after the end of the war somehow managed to avoid capture. Early in March 1946, he was run to ground in

Left: Demonstrations in Belgrade, autumn 1945, for the election of a constitutional assembly.

Below: Tito signs the proclamation abolishing the Monarchy and bringing the Republic into existence.

the hills near Višegrad and carried off to Belgrade to stand trial for high treason.

In May, while the prosecution were preparing the case against him, Tito set out on another state visit to Moscow. To all appearances it was an unqualified success. There were no allusions to past differences. Stalin was jocular, flattering, convivial, benevolent even. "Tito," he said, "should take care of himself and see that nothing happens to him. I have not much longer to live and he will remain for Europe."

Early in June, immediately after Tito's return from Moscow, Mihajlović was brought to trial. He was charged with high treason, collaboration with the enemy, and numerous war crimes. His trial, which lasted over a month, was made the occasion of repeated attacks on the British and American Governments, who were represented as having egged him on against the Partisans. While admitting that certain of his subordinates had reached accommodations with the enemy, Mihajlović denied all charges of terrorism and repeated that his purpose had been to organize resistance to the Axis. "I wanted much," he said in his final speech. "I began much, but the gale of the world carried me and my work away." On 15 July he was found guilty of war crimes and collaboration with the enemy and sentenced to be shot, the sentence being carried out two days later. It was, said Tito in a speech at Cetinje, "a sentence on international reaction."

Two months later, in September 1946, came the arrest and trial of Archbishop Stepinac, the Catholic archbishop of Zagreb and head of the Catholic hierarchy in Croatia, with whom the new regime had found themselves in conflict ever since they had come to power. When his trial opened in Zagreb on 30 September, the archbishop was charged with collaboration with the Germans and Italians and with the Ustaša, complicity in their crimes, and resistance to the new Government of Yugoslavia. In his defense, Stepinac, who had quite often found himself in opposition to the Ustaša, sought to justify the dealings he had had with them and with the Germans and denied complicity in their crimes. His conscience, he said, was clear. He also put the Church's side of the case and gave details of Communist persecution of Catholic clergy and congregations. Inevitably he was found guilty on the charges brought against him and sentenced to sixteen years' hard labor.

With any potential opponents safely out of the way, Tito turned his attention to the war-shattered economy, launching in November 1946 an ambitious Five Year Plan designed to industrialize the new Yugoslavia and make her economically self-sufficient. Particular emphasis was placed on heavy industry. The value of industrial production was to increase by 223 percent, the national income by 93 percent. And so on. The necessary industrial equipment and raw materials would come from the Soviet Union and the other countries of the Eastern bloc which had been formed since the war with Soviet leadership.

As a Communist, Tito was naturally determined to bring under state ownership the means of production, distribution, and exchange and to do it as soon as possible. "For us," he said, "the most dangerous thing of all would be to stop halfway." In December 1946 laws were passed nationalizing industry, commerce, trade, insurance, banking, transport, and communications. Less simple was the nationalization or collectivization of all agricultural land. The peasants proved as stubborn as Tito himself. The Government could arrest them or seize their land or impose quotas. It could not make them produce food against their will, and without food the life of the country could not go on. Soon a battle was engaged, marked by retreats and advances on both sides, which Tito, like Stalin before him, was to find an extremely exacting one.

Within two years Tito and his comrades had advanced further toward their ideal of a Communist state than any other country in the Soviet bloc. They also found themselves in the front line of the Cold War now being waged between East and West, between Russia and her East European dependencies on the one hand and the Western democracies on the other. Nothing Tito had done had endeared him to Western public opinion, which, shocked by his totalitarian tendencies and apparent subservience to Moscow, had already begun to forget his brave fight against the common enemy during the war. Trieste had become a danger point where the forces of

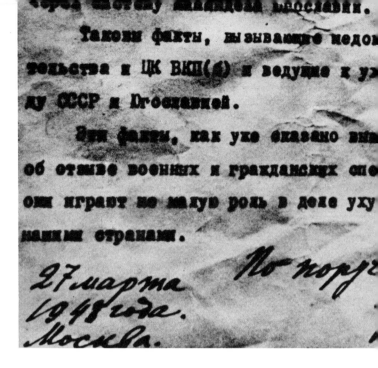

East and West faced each other angrily across a few strands of barbed wire.

It was against this explosive background that in August 1946 came the news that an unarmed American transport aircraft, which had strayed across the frontier in a storm, had been fired on and forced down by Yugoslav fighters. It was followed a few days later by the news that a second American transport had been attacked and this time shot down with the loss of all on board. Protests were exchanged. Tension increased. Tito reinforced his troops on the frontier. Then more prudent counsels prevailed. The Yugoslavs expressed regret. The crew of the first aircraft were set free and compensation offered. But this could not bring the dead airmen back and in the United States Tito became still more unpopular.

In Greece, meanwhile, a war was being fought by the Greek army against substantial Communist guerrilla forces, by now in possession of much of Greek Macedonia and known to be receiving substantial help from Yugoslavia. Here the Cold War had turned into a shooting war and again Yugoslavia was well to the fore. When in the autumn of 1947 it was announced that Belgrade had been chosen by Moscow as the seat of the newly created Cominform or Communist Information Bureau, it came as a surprise to no one.

But beneath the surface things were not quite what they seemed. There were signs, for instance, that Tito's economic policy did not enjoy the wholehearted approval of the Soviet Union, that Moscow did not want to see Yugoslavia industrialized and self-sufficient, but would rather keep her undeveloped, as a source of raw materials, as part of the Soviet economic empire.

"What do you want with a heavy industry?" asked one high Soviet official. "We have everything you need in the Urals." Nor did the Kremlin only disapprove of Yugoslavia's policies. Since the end of the war Tito, resplendent in his Marshal's uniform, had paid a series of visits to the other countries of Eastern Europe. Wherever he went he had been acclaimed. He had used these visits and those he received in return to discuss mutual problems and conclude mutual arrangements, without always asking permission of Moscow. There had been, for example, talk of a Balkan Federation. To Stalin's

suspicious mind, such conduct was not desirable on the part of satellites. The time, he decided, had come to establish closer control over these new outposts of empire.

The purpose of the Cominform, as its name indicated, was to facilitate "the exchange of information" between Communist parties and coordinate their policy "on a basis of mutual agreement." The decision to establish it in Belgrade had been taken by Stalin himself. Soon it became clear that, apart from collecting intelligence from one source or another, one function of Comrade Yudin, the permanent Soviet representative, was to make trouble between Yugoslavia and her Cominform partners. Meanwhile the same thing was being done at a higher level.

In January 1948 Milovan Djilas and Koča Popović were suddenly summoned to Moscow and informed by Stalin that Yugoslavia was "free to swallow Albania whenever she chose," the invitation being accompanied by a crude but expressive gesture. What could this mean? Slightly nonplussed, the Yugoslavs raised the perennial question of their country's need for military supplies. "We will give you everything you need," countered Stalin expansively. But after that nothing happened and they were left to cool their heels for a month. Complications, they were told, had arisen.

At the end of January events took a new and dramatic turn. A Yugoslav-Bulgarian Treaty of Friendship and Mutual Assistance had been signed, with Moscow's approval, in November 1947. Following this a statement by Georgi Dimitrov, now back in his native Bulgaria, on the subject of a possible Balkan Federation had apparently infuriated Stalin. Dimitrov, having at once retracted his statement, was called to Moscow. Tito, also summoned, preferred to send Kardelj and Vladimir Bakarić from Croatia to join Djilas.

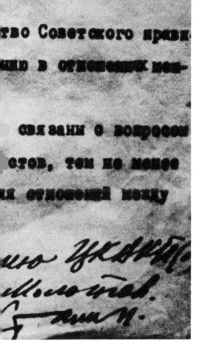

The note of 27 March 1948 signed by Stalin and Molotov, informing the Yugoslavs that they were liars and comparing them with Trotski and Bukharin, left no doubt that the fight was on. The threatening letter from Moscow marked the lowest point in relations between Yugoslavia and the Soviet Union, and led to the definitive break with Russia.

And now, before Kardelj and Bakarić could reach Moscow, came more trouble. In response to a request from Tirana the Yugoslavs had readily agreed to send the Albanians two divisions to help defend their southern borders against Greece, when a message arrived from Moscow declaring that, unless the arrangement was immediately canceled, the Yugoslavs would be publicly denounced. Coming on top of Stalin's invitation to Djilas to "swallow Albania," Moscow's latest reaction was frankly mystifying. It began to look as though serious trouble were brewing.

A meeting held in the Kremlin on 10 February 1948, with both Yugoslav and Bulgarian delegations present, abundantly confirmed this. While Stalin sat scowling, Molotov opened the proceedings. Serious differences, he said, had arisen between the Soviet Union on the one hand, and Yugoslavia and Bulgaria on the other, differences "inadmissible both from a Party and from a State point of view." From time to time Stalin broke in with surly and sardonic observations. When Kardelj and Dimitrov tried to excuse themselves, he became even angrier, flatly contradicting them and brushing aside their excuses. There were differences between them, he kept repeating, big differences. Then he told them what he wanted: three federations: Hungary and Roumania; Poland and Czechoslovakia; Yugoslavia and Bulgaria. "The time," he said, "is ripe. Bulgaria and Yugoslavia must unite immediately. Then they must annex Albania." Both delegations were then told they must sign an agreement providing for mutual consultation with the Kremlin on all questions of foreign policy.

Talking it over afterward Kardelj, Bakarić, and Djilas agreed that they must at all costs resist the demand for immediate federation with Bulgaria, which was clearly a Soviet device for gaining control of Yugoslavia. Having reluctantly signed the agreement for mutual consultation, they returned, unnerved, to Belgrade to report to Tito.

By now the signs of trouble were multiplying. From Bucharest came the news that Tito's portraits were being taken down. In Moscow the Soviet Ministry of Foreign Trade abruptly broke off negotiations for a new trade agreement, virtually putting an end to Soviet-Yugoslav trade. Clearly Soviet-Yugoslav relations were approaching a crisis.

How had this happened? Before the war Tito's relations with Moscow had presented no problem. He had simply done as he was told. Since then a lot had happened. With many thousands of his fellow-countrymen Tito had undergone the hazards and hardships of a savage, bitter war. He had built up from nothing a formidable military and political machine. He had tasted the triumph of ultimate victory. Human experience shapes human character. It would have been surprising if, after all this, Tito had been as ready as ever to take his orders from a foreign master. More than once he had found himself disagreeing with Moscow. At one time that would have been unthinkable. To the Russians it still was. But, after what they had achieved, the Yugoslavs had come to believe in working things out for themselves. There has been much speculation as to the cause of Tito's dispute with Moscow. Its subject or occasion was secondary. What mattered was that there should be a dispute at all. The Soviet system was based on the absolute and infallible authority of the Kremlin. Tito, on a number of issues, was challenging that authority. And this was something which Stalin was not prepared to tolerate.

In what was clearly a critical situation Tito turned, as always, to the Party, the Party which he had built up and on which his power was founded. Summoning the Central Committee to his villa in Dedinje on 1 March, he told them that Soviet-Yugoslav relations had reached a deadlock. After due discussion they agreed that the Soviet demand for immediate federation with Bulgaria must be resisted. The Bulgarians were Soviet puppets. To accept union with Bulgaria would be to admit a Trojan Horse to their midst. The independence of Yugoslavia was at stake.

While outwardly all remained calm, Soviet pressure was now suddenly intensified. All Soviet military advisers were withdrawn on the ground that they were "surrounded by hostility." They were followed a day or two later by their civilian counterparts. Tito decided to address himself to Molotov direct. In a note dated 20 March 1948 he said that he and his colleagues were "surprised and hurt" by the action of the Soviet Government and asked to be "told straight out" what the trouble was.

The Soviet reply was handed to Tito by the Soviet ambassador just over a week later. It consisted of eight closely typed pages and left him in no doubt at all what the trouble was. "We consider your answer," it began, "untruthful and therefore wholly unsatisfactory." It went on in the same sneering, menacing tone, denouncing the leaders of the Yugoslav Party as hostile to the Soviet Union, ideologically unsound, and out of sympathy with their own rank and file, comparing them to Trotski and Bukharin and accusing them of deliberately keeping an English spy in their midst. It was, in effect, a declaration of war which at its foot bore not only the signature of Molotov, but that of Stalin himself, giving it the weight and sanctity of holy writ.

After drafting a reply and showing it to Kardelj, Djilas, Ranković, and Kidrič, who agreed that they must stand firm, Tito called a further meeting of the Central Committee for 12 April and put the issue squarely to them. "This," he said, "is not a matter of theoretical discussion or ideological errors. The issue at stake is the relationship between one state and another." Kardelj and those who followed him agreed with Tito. There was only one dissentient voice. Black Žujović came down heavily on the side of the Soviet Union, whereat he was promptly expelled from the committee. Its members then set to work on Tito's reply. In its final form it remained as uncompromising as ever, categorically denying every Soviet accusation and blandly announcing that "however much each of us loves the Soviet Union, he can in no way love his own country less."

Tito now knew that, with the exception of Žujović, already eliminated, he could rely on the leadership of the Party. Their reactions had been the same as his own. Their first loyalty was to their country and not to Moscow. The Russians had failed to drive a wedge between him and the little group of men who had been through so much with him.

Things could not remain where they were. Stalin's next move was to mobilize the other Cominform countries. During the second half of April, communications, in terms similar to the Soviet note, were received from the Czech, Hungarian, Roumanian, Bulgarian, and Polish parties. These were followed on 4 May by a further twenty-five page note from Stalin and Molotov in which they repeated all their earlier charges and added a number of new ones, notably that, apart from their ideological deviations, the Yugoslav leaders were "boundlessly arrogant," undemocratic in their methods, and ridiculously conceited about their alleged exploits during the war.

Nothing could have been better calculated to unite the Yugoslav Party behind Tito than these aspersions on Yugoslavia's wartime achievements. In a short reply, drafted on 9 May, the Central Committee flatly rejected the Soviet suggestion that the right body to deal with the dispute was the Cominform, well known to be heavily weighted against them. They then decreed that Žujović and Andrija Hebrang from Croatia, formerly president of the State Planning Committee and also well known to have close links with Moscow, should be expelled from the Party and arrested on a charge of high treason.

Disregarding the Yugoslav refusal to attend, the Russians now proceeded with their proposal that Yugoslavia's misdemeanors should be discussed at a meeting of the Cominform in Bucharest, and on 28 June the text of a resolution passed on this occasion was abruptly published in Prague. It began with a scathing denunciation of Tito and the other Yugoslav leaders, recounting at length their ideological deviations, their hostility to the Soviet Union, their "boundless ambition, arrogance, and conceit" and the "Turkish and terroristic" character of their regime. It ended with a direct invitation to the rank and file of the Yugoslav Party to rid themselves of their leaders. There could no longer be any doubt about it. The fight was on.

After reading the Cominform resolution, Tito spent a couple of hours pacing up and down the room. He had reached the parting of the ways. Inevitably it would now be the aim of the Kremlin to wipe him out. His immediate problem was how to survive.

Next day he called a further meeting of the Central Committee, who showed no signs of weakening, and passed a resolution firmly rebutting the Cominform's charges and calling the Party to close its ranks. At the same time they decided to publish the main documents involved in the Yugoslav press. Next morning all over the country seething crowds struggled to buy copies of *Borba* and learn of the breach, the incredible breach with Moscow. As it happened, there were just three weeks left before the date of the next Party congress, the fifth since its foundation and the first since it had assumed power. How would the rank and file of the Party react to what had happened? What view would its five hundred thousand

The threat from Moscow of 27 March was followed by a further serious attack on Tito and the Yugoslav leaders. This was the Resolution of the meeting of the Cominform in Bucharest in June, which made grave accusations: "Hostility to the Soviet Union," and "boundless ambitions, arrogance…"

By their reactions to Tito's eight-hour speech at the Fifth Party Congress on 21 July 1948, the audience made it abundantly clear that he could count on their support against Soviet pressure.

The break with the Kremlin was now complete, despite Stalin's warning: "I will shake my little finger—and there will be no more Tito." Stalin is seen here glorified in a Soviet painting.

After his break with Stalin, then at the height of his power, Tito soon succeeded in establishing friendly relations with the Western democracies. Right: Tito on his visit to London, 1953.

members take of this sudden break with the Country of the Revolution, so long held up to them as the source of all wisdom and virtue? For Tito everything depended on this. The first necessity, if he was to survive, was to carry the Party and the country with him.

The omens, on the whole, were favorable. In the Party there was pained indignation at the attitude of the Cominform and among non-Communists a new admiration for Tito's robust attitude toward the Russians. Even so it was essential that he should tread warily and lend no substance to the charges brought against him by Cominform.

Opening the Congress on 21 July 1948, he first recalled what he and the other leaders of the Party had done over the last ten years to inculcate and instill in its members "a spirit of deep trust, love, and devotion toward the Soviet Union, the Country of Progress, the Country of Socialism, the Protector of Small Peoples." He spoke, too, of the Party's achievements during the ten years for which he had been its leader. It was only at the very end of a speech which had already lasted for almost eight hours that he "turned briefly" to the Cominform and their "monstrous accusations," nevertheless declaring that it was his firm intention to restore good relations with the Soviet Party.

When at last he sat down to shouts of "Stalin! Tito!," he had achieved a lot. He had reminded his listeners of all that he himself had done for the Party and for Yugoslavia. He had recalled their wartime comradeship. He had also refuted the charges brought against him and aroused the wrath of his audience against those who had made them. Nor had he once been openly provocative. "I had," he said afterward, "to give Stalin time to behave in such a way that people in Yugoslavia would say 'Down with Stalin!' of their own accord without my having to suggest it to them." All in all it had been a remarkable performance. Tito had shown that he was master in his own house, with the Party solidly behind him, while the Cominform's invitation to get rid of him had been indignantly flung back in their teeth.

From the Kremlin's point of view things could scarcely have been worse. Stalin had clearly been led to suppose that Tito would not be hard to get rid of. "I will shake my little finger,"

he said to Khrushchev, "and there will be no more Tito." But it had not worked out like that. As the months went by, it became clear that Tito was unlikely to succumb to purely political pressure. Since June the Kremlin had let loose against him the full fury of their propaganda machine, denouncing his as a Fascist, a murderer, a lackey of the Imperialists. They had also tried to infiltrate the Party. But neither Žujović nor Hebrang had been quick enough. Tito, an old hand at such matters, had liquidated them before they could liquidate him. General Arso Jovanović, a former chief of staff, had, it was announced, been shot on the Roumanian frontier while trying to defect to Russia. There had been no other defectors of any consequence.

At his best in a crisis, Tito gave during these critical months the impression of a man supremely sure of himself, as calm, resolute, and resilient as he had ever been. The decision to defy the Kremlin had, he admitted, not been an easy one. "But now that it's taken," he said to the present author, "I've never been gladder of anything in my life." Already he felt sure enough of his position to admit that his quarrel was with Stalin personally, adding with the utmost confidence that he was right and Stalin wrong.

The dilemma now confronting Moscow was a serious one. Tito was openly challenging the authority of the Kremlin and challenging it with impunity. If the Soviet Government were not to suffer a disastrous loss of face, if they were not to risk the recurrence of the trouble elsewhere, Tito must by one means or another be obliterated. The Kremlin first resorted to an all-out economic blockade. Since the end of the war

Yugoslavia's economy had been firmly oriented toward the East, depending almost entirely on Russia and her satellites for markets, raw materials, capital equipment, consumer goods, and technical advice. Suddenly all this dried up.

It was a situation which called for steady nerves and an agile mind. Tito had both. A position of total isolation between East and West, of equal hostility to both, was clearly not practical politics, still less practical economics. Possibly Tito had from the first been sustained in his resistance to Soviet pressure by the thought that there was after all an alternative, by the recollection of his wartime relationship with the West. Even so, the transition would not be easy. He had no reason to assume that the Western democracies, on whom for three years he had heaped every insult and affront, would welcome him with open arms. Nor, having broken with Moscow to preserve his country's independence, could he logically sacrifice that independence to buy help from the capitalist West. Meanwhile the economic facts stared him relentlessly in the face. What Tito needed most was financial and economic aid to fill the void left by the Soviet economic boycott. This, he found on enquiry, the Western democracies were prepared to grant him, without, as he had feared, seeking to impose any political conditions. By the middle of 1949 it had become clear that the Soviet economic blockade was inlikely to achieve its object.

For a whole year now Tito had defied Stalin with impunity. Political and economic pressure had failed. Assassination, if it had been attempted, had not succeeded. There remained armed invasion. By the summer of 1949 the Russians were undoubtedly weighing up the pros and cons of such a course. The trouble was that they had waited too long. And the longer they waited, the greater the risk became. In June 1948 a sudden attack might have taken Tito unawares. Now he had had time to prepare. Nor could the Russians any longer be sure that Yugoslavia, if attacked, would stand alone. Imperceptibly, despite ideological differences, a better understanding was growing up between Tito and the Western democracies, by now themselves more aware of the Soviet menace and, since the signature of the North Atlantic Treaty, better prepared to meet it.

With British and American help Tito now reequipped his armed forces and before long could put into the field thirty well-armed, well-trained divisions. Soon the rapprochement was carried a stage further. In March 1953 Tito paid an official visit to Great Britain, his first to any foreign country since 1948. Accompanied by Koča Popović, now state secretary for foreign affairs, he lunched with the Queen at Buckingham Palace and dined with Mr. Churchill at No. 10 Downing Street. The visit was an undoubted success. "We really knew," he said, "that we had come to a friendly and allied country…we found a common language in all matters…. We were treated as equals and not with the arrogance we saw in the East."

In the East… Early in March 1953, while Tito was on his way to London, death had come to his adversary and former leader, Josif Vissarionovich Djugashvili, better known as Stalin. Tito's quarrel, or so the story went, had been with Stalin. And now, with Stalin out of the way, came indications

After Stalin's death in March 1953 there were signs of a changed attitude on Moscow's part. There ensued, on 25 May 1955, a visit by Khrushchev to Belgrade. In his speech at the airport (below) he declared: "We sincerely regret what happened."

With time Tito was able to establish a relatively friendly relationship with Khrushchev, who could be cheerful enough when it suited him.

that the new rulers of the Soviet Union were anxious to let bygones be bygones and, in the phrase then current, to "coexist" with Tito. Tito's reaction, not surprisingly, was one of extreme caution. After due consideration, he agreed to the reappointment of ambassadors and the resumption of trade negotiations. But no more. This was in no way a return to the relationship which had existed before 1948. "We are," said Tito, "quite competent to recognize a trap." Nor had he any intention of sacrificing his new friendship with the West. "These," he said, "proved in difficult times to be not our enemies but our friends. We cannot let the good relations we have built up with them deteriorate, simply for the sake of better relations with the Eastern bloc."

But the Russians persisted. From Moscow, where Khrushchev and Bulganin now held sway, came in the spring of 1955 a cordial invitation to visit them there. To this Tito, without undue enthusiasm, replied that, while unwilling to go to Moscow, he was nevertheless prepared to receive Khrushchev and Bulganin in Belgrade. Bulganin, it is true, had described him as "a Judas" and "a contemptible traitor," while Khrushchev had called him "a Fascist" and his government "a gang of hired Anglo-American spies and murderers." Even so he was prepared to be magnanimous—up to a point. The visit began on the afternoon of 25 May when Khrushchev

and Bulganin landed at Belgrade airport. Correct and impassive in his Marshal's uniform, Tito was waiting to receive them. "Everything," said Khrushchev reassuringly as he scrambled out of the aeroplane, "is going to be all right." Having hurriedly inspected the guard of honor, he then planted himself in front of a microphone and embarked on a prolonged apology for Russia's past treatment of Yugoslavia. It had all, he said, been a terrible mistake. "We sincerely regret what happened," he went on. The trouble stemmed from "acts of provocation" committed by "enemies of the people," now unmasked. In future the Soviet Party would do all they could to reestablish mutual understanding with their Yugoslav comrades. Together, the two parties must "throw off the yoke of capitalism." "Long live Tito," he concluded, "Long live Yugoslavia," then, stepping back, offered Tito the

microphone. But Tito, impassive as ever, simply motioned him to where a car was waiting to take them up to Dedinje. In the streets the crowds cheered Tito, ignoring the Russians. The visit lasted just over a week, ending, after a series of formal meetings interspersed with official receptions, with an innocuous Joint Declaration of Friendship and Cooperation, dwelling mainly on "peace-loving principles" but also stressing that the internal and ideological affairs of each country were that country's own business.

From his trial of strength with the Soviet Union Tito had emerged not only unscathed but triumphant. It had been the Russians who had come to Belgrade to make amends and sue for peace and who, abandoning their claims to ideological infallibility, had accepted him on his own terms as an independent Communist.

During the years that followed their break with Moscow the Yugoslavs had plenty of time to take stock of their ideological position. It would perhaps be too much to say that a new ideology was created to suit a new situation. But the crisis they had passed through certainly helped clarify and crystallize their ideas. "The Yugoslav brand of Communism," said Tito, "was not something imported from Moscow, but had its origin in the woods and forests of Yugoslavia." During the war the Yugoslav Communists had got into the habit of working things out for themselves. It was a habit that was to persist in peacetime.

Already by 1952 there were signs of a new spirit abroad, of an all-round relaxation of controls. There was less interference by the State in people's lives. The security police faded into the background. People began to enjoy themselves more. And at sixty Tito, as though to set an example, having divorced his wartime wife Herta, married Jovanka Budisavljević, a handsome Serbian girl in her twenties.

In the economy the emphasis was now on decentralization, enterprise, initiative, the profit motive. The theory behind these new policies was that the central bureaucracy should relinquish its hold on the nationalized industries and hand over control to the workers. This, it was explained, was a first step toward the withering away of the State, as foretold by Karl Marx. Under a basic law passed in June 1950 economic enterprises were to be owned and managed by the producers. In agriculture the Government first abandoned the policy of trying to force peasants into collective farms and then gave permission for peasants already collectivized to leave their cooperatives. Soon over eighty percent of the land was again under private ownership. Meanwhile Yugoslavia was thrown wide open to foreign visitors and more and more Yugoslavs began to travel abroad.

These new trends received the formal blessing of the Party at its Sixth Congress, held in Zagreb in November 1952. The resolutions had been drafted by Milovan Djilas, now the Party's chief dialectician, who, from a hard liner, has become a leading proponent of liberalization. The Russians, the assembled delegates were told, had betrayed Socialism and degenerated into the worst kind of imperialists and state

Today there are two main systems in the world, the socialist and the capitalist. But this certainly does not mean that there cannot be constructive cooperation between them in all questions which are of interest to the peoples of individual countries.

Tito, at the great rally in Moscow, 19 June 1956.

At the invitation of the new Soviet leadership, Tito visited Russia in June 1956 in a completely altered atmosphere. Enthusiastic crowds greeted him everywhere.

Below: *The great stadium in Moscow during Tito's speech on 19 June.*

Bottom: *Tito and Kardelj (at right) in talks with the Soviet leaders.*

capitalists. Having successfully shaken off the "terrible delusion" under which they had once labored, the Yugoslav Party were now the only true exponents of Marxism–Leninism. To emphasize this, the Party now changed its name, its statutes, and, in theory, its functions, becoming the Communist League, a part of the larger Socialist Alliance. From executive, its role would henceforth become advisory and educational. "From now on," said Djilas, "the Party line is that there is no Party line," while Tito went even further, observing that "if the State really withers away the Party must necessarily wither away with it." Two months later, in January 1953, the old Soviet-style constitution was replaced by a new constitution, diminishing the authority of the central government, giving more power to the Republican and local authorities, and establishing the office of President of the Republic, to which Tito was at once elected.

It was against this background that in October 1953 a series of articles by Djilas began to appear in *Borba*, the official Party organ, in which the author, who, with Kardelj and Ranković, ranked immediately after Tito in the Yugoslav hierarchy, set out to survey the future of the Party. In them he spoke of the new ideas which were to "transform" the Revolution. "The only possibility," he wrote, "is more democracy, more free discussion, freer elections." And Tito, while saying that he did not agree with everything in them, told him, when asked for his opinion, to "go on writing." There were others, Kardelj for instance, who were less enthusiastic. But Djilas, dismissing his critics as "Stalinist bureaucrats," went on writing. At the New Year three of his articles appeared in a single issue. Special meetings were held to discuss them. Public opinion was in a ferment, the reaction being largely favorable.

But if some of the rank and file liked Djilas's articles, the upper echelons of the Party did not. A crisis was inevitable. Djilas precipitated it by publishing a savagely satirical sketch of life in higher Party circles and their "pseudo-aristocratic" pretensions. The Party hierarchy, with its womenfolk to the fore, turned on him like tigers. Djilas was publicly denounced by the Central Committee and orders given for a Party enquiry.

The enquiry opened in Belgrade on 16 January 1954 and lasted ten days. Tito, who spoke first, did his best to make things easy for Djilas; Kardelj and Moša Pijade were less kind. Djilas himself was confused, but more or less contrite. He was nevertheless expelled from the Central Committee of the Party and obliged to resign from his government posts.

The Djilas crisis served to focus attention on a fundamental problem, namely how to reconcile the authoritarian character of the regime with the new policy of liberalism and decentralization which had received official sanction at the Sixth Party Congress. The struggle, as Kardelj put it, had to be waged on two fronts: against anarchy on the one hand and bureaucracy on the other. It was a problem which would continue to exercise the rulers of the new Yugoslavia for years to come. One thing, however, was certain. There was no room in Tito's scheme of things for a Leader of the Opposition, the role in which Djilas seemed to see himself. Toward the end of December a further crisis provoked by an interview with *The New York Times* led to his prosecution and to a suspended sentence of eighteen months.

Abroad as well as at home, in foreign as well as in domestic policy, Tito's greatest skill lay in his ability to keep a proper balance between two extremes. For five or six years now he had enjoyed excellent relations with the West. In June 1956, in response to a pressing invitation from the new Soviet leaders, he agreed to return their visit of the year before. It was ten years since he had been to Moscow. Then he had come as a satellite; this time as an equal. That February Khrushchev had, with his famous speech to the Twentieth Party Congress, carried the process of de-Stalinization a stage further, dwelling at length on Stalin's "shameful" and "monstrous" treatment of Yugoslavia. In April the Cominform had been abolished. The day before Tito's arrival Molotov, co-signatory with Stalin of those ominous notes of 1948, had been summarily dismissed.

But perhaps the most significant thing of all was the welcome Tito received from the Russian people. Everywhere he went, grinning broadly in his powder-blue Marshal's uniform, in Moscow, in Leningrad, at Stalingrad and Sochi, he was the center of an immense cheering crowd of ordinary Russians, cheering, not their government's official guest, but the rebel, the man who had defied the Kremlin and got away with it, the man who, after pausing briefly before Lenin's coffin in his mausoleum on the Red Square, had turned contemptuously away from the glass case next to it, the case which contained the mortal remains of his former adversary, J. V. Stalin.

Such a triumph might have turned a lesser man's head. Tito kept his. He went, it is true, quite a long way, agreeing this time to the resumption of fraternal relations between Parties and speaking of "a broad similarity of views" on a number of topics. But there was all the difference between this and actual adherence to a bloc. His strength, he knew, lay in his "nonalignment" and that he was determined to maintain, indeed to extend, if possible, to others. At the Twentieth Party Congress in February Khrushchev had enunciated a new doctrine which had originated with Tito and was embodied in the joint communiqué issued at the end of Tito's visit, the doctrine of different roads to Socialism. This, if it meant anything, signified that the Kremlin had abandoned its claim to infallibility and universality. "There are," said Tito confidently on his way through Bucharest, "no more satellites."

The truth, as he was soon to discover, was rather different. Inevitably Tito's example, the triumphant vindication of his revolt, had had its effect on the satellites. So had Khrushchev's drastic demolition of the Stalin legend. For the first time in thirty years a wind of change was blowing through the Communist world. From the Pandora's box which Stalin's successors had so imprudently opened, all kinds of strange shapes were emerging. That same summer serious rioting broke out at Poznan in Poland. "Down with the Russians!" cried the rioters. Clearly the brake would need to be applied. If Khrushchev had ever meant what he said about different roads to Socialism, he now had second thoughts. To the Communist Parties of all the satellites a secret circular was now dispatched warning them against the Yugoslavs and reminding them that the Soviet Union remained the "directing Party" and only true example for Communist movements worldwide.

Wladyslav Gomulka was reelected Secretary of the Polish Communist Party in 1956. "Every country," he said, "has the right to be independent."

To this repudiation of a vital principle Tito reacted violently and in September Khrushchev came hurrying to Yugoslavia on a private visit, which Tito returned ten days later. They were photographed together at the seaside. "Did the Yugoslavs give way?" asked a journalist. "The Yugoslavs are not in the habit of giving way," came the answer.

But by now theoretical discussions were fast being overtaken by events. In mid-October the reemergence of Wladyslaw Gomulka, a previous Secretary of the Polish Party discarded on Russian instructions, and other dramatic changes in the Polish Politburo caused Khrushchev to fly at short notice to Warsaw. "I'll show you the Road to Socialism," he yelled. "If you don't do what you're told, we'll wipe you out by force." But the Poles stood firm and Gomulka, reelected Secretary of the Party, became a national hero and a symbol of resistance to Russia. "Every country," he declared, "has the right to be independent."

More serious still was the rising which, after some talk of liberalization, broke out a few days later in Hungary, bringing to power a government who boldly declared Hungary's independence, neutrality, and attachment to the democratic freedoms. This, Khrushchev quickly realized, was no time for half-measures. Budapest was surrounded by a dozen Soviet divisions and, after much fierce fighting, the rebellion ruthlessly crushed.

From these events, Tito, as hard-headed as ever, drew two conclusions: first that, when necessary, Khrushchev was prepared to use armed force and, secondly, that what started as a liberalizing movement could easily get out of hand. He did not want his country to be overrun by the Russians. Nor did he want to be liberalized out of office. From sympathetic, his attitude toward Hungary became noncommittal. And when Milovan Djilas criticized him for this in an American magazine, he promptly sent him to jail.

Meanwhile the Russians had drawn their own conclusions from what had happened. Recent events had shaken the au-

Tito's successful resistance against Moscow's domination encouraged some of the Soviet satellites to assert their right to independence and to seek their own route to Socialism. There were rebellions in Poland and, most dramatically, in Hungary in autumn 1956. The Budapest uprising (at left is a tank with rebels, and a flag without a star) was ruthlessly crushed by a dozen Soviet Army divisions and much of Budapest was reduced to ruins.

thority of the Kremlin inside and outside the Soviet Union and in their eyes the responsibility for this lay fairly and squarely with Tito. Abruptly the Soviet-Yugoslav honeymoon came to an end. Again Tito became a target for hostile Soviet propoganda and in return gave as good as he got.

But Tito, once more on bad terms with the East and not wishing to commit himself too wholeheartedly to the capitalist West, had hit on another alternative. Yugoslavia was not the only country in the world that was trying to assert her independence, to establish a position of "nonalignment" between the big power blocs. The emerging Third World was full of former dependencies of the colonial powers now seeking to make their way in the world and also offering potential sources of raw materials and markets for Yugoslav exports. Returning from a visit to India, Ethiopia, and Egypt in 1955, Tito had declared that the uncommitted countries were Yugoslavia's "true allies and greatest friends." In 1956 he held

The Conference of Non-aligned Nations in Belgrade (below). In the activity of the uncommitted countries the Belgrade Conference had a special significance. It rallied the greatest number of leading national representatives to gather up to then, chiefs of states and governments of 25 countries from various continents, of various nationalities, races, and colors. The Conference which attracted world attention, sat in the capital of Yugoslavia from 1 to 6 September 1961.

a meeting on the island of Brioni with President Nasser of Egypt and President Nehru of India. It marked, in a sense, the beginning of the Nonaligned Movement, whose first formal conference was held in Belgrade in 1961.

Right: The Non-aligned Movement held its first conference in the Parliament building in the Yugoslav capital. It ended with a joint resolution on the main problems of the world today.

Left: *The meeting of Presidents Nasser, Nehru, and Tito in 1956 marked the birth of the Non-aligned Movement.*

... We have met at a serious moment and the present days have a fateful influence upon the future of world peace. Our material forces are modest, and our possibilities far from unlimited, yet our moral powers are enormous and this today is in itself a great force.

.... Underdeveloped countries do not ask for charity. They have a right to assistance on principles which will make possible for them an even faster and more varied development.

Tito in his speech on 3 September 1961

During the years that followed, Soviet-Yugoslav relations settled into a pattern which was to repeat itself with uncanny regularity. A reconciliation in 1957 was quickly followed by another sharp deterioration. In June 1958 Khrushchev angrily denounced Tito as a "Trojan Horse" and declared that the Cominform Resolution of ten years before had been "fundamentally correct." Three years later, in 1961, came signs of an improvement. Visits were exchanged by the Soviet and Yugoslav foreign ministers and in September of that year the first World Conference of nonaligned nations held under Tito's auspices in Belgrade pleased the Russians by the resolutely anti-Western tone of its proceedings. In the summer of 1962 Khrushchev actually spoke of Yugoslavia as "building Socialism" and described Soviet-Yugoslav relations as "normal, even good." Later President Leonid Brezhnev visited Belgrade and Tito returned his visit.

Thereafter there was a steady improvement in relations between the two countries which coincided with a corresponding cooling of Yugoslavia's relations with the West. In 1963 Khrushchev visited Tito on Brioni, where the two had long talks together, discussing among other things Yugoslavia's experiments in self-management. "What did he think of them?" the present author enquired of Tito some weeks later. "He was much impressed," came the ready answer. "In fact he said he was going straight back to do the same thing in Russia."

Foreign policy was for Tito an area of especial activity. He visited and received heads of state from all over the world: Tito as the guest of the Queen of England (above), Tito given a triumphal welcome in North

Korea (below), Tito in discussion with the President of the United States, Jimmy Carter (right), discussions with President Giscard d'Estaing of France (below left), Tito receiving a visit from Brezhnev (below center), and also from West German Chancellor Willi Brandt. The illustrations on this page portray a small selection of Tito's diplomatic encounters. Of equally great significance were his connections with the leading personalities of the Third World. The leader of little Yugoslavia had become a force in world politics.

But this was not to be. Not many months later came Khrushchev's fall from power and his replacement as Party Secretary by Leonid Brezhnev. To Tito, who had over the years established a not unfriendly relationship with Khrushchev, his abrupt disappearance caused a moment of anxiety. But on visiting the Soviet Union in June 1965, he was warmly received by the new leadership and responded by a speech in which he declared that, in spite of past misunderstandings, no Yugoslav could doubt that "if difficult times were to come," his country would stand firmly on the side of the Soviet Union. It would nevertheless have been wrong to conclude on this account, as some observers did, that Yugoslavia had necessarily "disappeared behind the Iron Curtain."

Just as Tito took an independent line internationally, so Yugoslavia's domestic policies also had a character of their own. Here again, all his skill and judgment were required to keep the right balance between excessive restraint and excessive liberalism, to reconcile socialist planning with self-management, and to decide what the proper role of the Party should be in what, it was now claimed, was a grass-roots democracy. Bold social, political, and economic experiments remained the order of the day. "Nothing," the Party's 1958 program had declared, "should be so sacred that it cannot be transcended by something still freer and more human."

By encouraging "pluralism" and self-management, by allowing independent enterprises to dispose freely of their earnings, the rulers of the new Yugoslavia had, with their eyes wide open, brought into being any number of new interests which now needed to be taken into account. Decentralization had been almost too successful.

There were times when things went well, but times when they went less well. The boom of the nineteen-fifties was followed in 1961 by a serious recession, facing those responsible with the need for effective action. Some advocated more liberalization and decentralization and some less, while Tito kept a judicious balance between the two. More disturbing, in what was fast becoming a market economy, the debate had begun to assume nationalist overtones. Behind the question of economic decentralization loomed that of political devolution, aggravated by marked differences between the republics, in living standards and economic development.

To most people the answer seemed to lie in more decentralization. The new federal constitution of 1963, mainly the work of Edvard Kardelj, marked a further step in this direction and Kardelj and the Croat leader Bakarić, another advocate of decentralization, gained further ground at the Eighth Party Congress in December 1964, when Tito appeared to favor their point of view.

A strong proponent of central control, on the other hand, was

Below: *A meeting of the personnel of a large concern who are electing the worker council which in turn will elect members to additional administrative committees.*

Marko Ranković, Organizing Secretary of the Party, chief of security services, vice-president of the Republic, and Tito's most probable successor. From long experience he distrusted decentralization, whether economic or political, believing rather in strong Party and government control, concentrated in Belgrade, the capital of his native Serbia, and, as far as possible, in his own hands.

During the second half of 1965 it became apparent that the new program of increased economic decentralization launched that summer and known as the Reform was being held up by opposition from within the Party. This was something Tito could not tolerate, whoever was responsible. Action would have to be taken. As a first move, it would have been hard in choosing a scapegoat to pick a more popular target than UDBA, the security police, which ever since the war had been Ranković's personal domain. And now, in the early summer of 1966, rumors began to circulate than UDBA had been abusing their powers. Then on 9 June came the news that not only the houses and offices of various Ministers and senior members of the Party, but Tito's own office and residence had been secretly wired for sound. After some preliminary moves, the Central Committee of the Party were summoned to Brioni for a plenary meeting on 1 July.

105

The picture that emerged from their deliberations was a disturbing one. UDBA, it appeared, had indeed been exceeding their powers. Moreover. Ranković, their head, with all the special powers which that implied, was also Organizing Secretary of the Party, controlling all political appointments. In other words, "he had the entire Party in his hands" and was able, if he so wished, to reverse its decisions from within. "Doesn't this rather remind you of what went on under Stalin?" Tito asked.

Sharply attacked by his colleagues, Ranković, suddenly without a friend, assumed full moral and political responsibility for all that had happened and resigned from all his offices, after which he was expelled from the Party, demands for his arrest being rejected on account of his past services. Thereafter he kept himself to himself, living quietly on an adequate pension and taking no part in public life. Meanwhile Tito made it clear that he, for one, had not swung right over to the decentralizers. "I'm not joining up with any liberals!" he merrily announced to a group of Partisan veterans who visited him on Brioni a few days later.

The crisis had been surmounted, the danger overcome, and the balance between opposing factions skillfully redressed. Excessive power was no longer concentrated in any one man's hands. Ranković's posts and appointments were redistributed. From Tito's chosen successor and the second most powerful man in Yugoslavia, he was abruptly relegated to the same limbo to which Milovan Djilas had been consigned twelve years earlier for going too far in the opposite direction. Of three men who had once been closest to Tito, Djilas, Ranković, and Kardelj, only Kardelj now remained, able, sensible and reliable, but at fifty-six already a sick man. Henceforward Tito, now in his seventy-fifth year, would have to rely more than ever on himself. It was a prospect which he faced with the utmost confidence.

The next two years were not easy ones for Yugoslavia either at home or abroad. Despite the Reform of 1965, the state of the economy, plagued by high inflation, irregular growth, and growing unemployment, gave little cause for satisfaction. Nor was there much comfort in agriculture. In the world at large Soviet–United States relations had worsened, while

Yugoslavia's relations with the West left much to be desired. Even nonalignment, the basis of Tito's foreign policy, seemed to have lost much of its validity, when, at the time of the Arab-Israeli Six Day War of June 1967, he openly aligned himself with the Soviet Union. Meanwhile at home a lively debate continued regarding the true role of the Party. Had the time come for it to wither away? The last word rested with Tito. The political consciousness of the people, he declared in April 1967, was still far below the level at which the Party could safely start shedding its attributes or diminishing its role. Democratic centralism must remain its watchword.

These years were nevertheless marked by a variety of political and economic experiments and a genuine dispersal of power and authority, described by one acute observer as polycentric polyarchy. The 1967 elections, fought on a multi-candidate basis, produced some surprising results, while in intellectual circles there was talk of a New Left, a Humanist Intelligentsia, Creative Marxism, and Marxist Humanism, all concepts well

beyond the bounds of Party orthodoxy. More worrying still were signs of reviving Croat nationalism. In Yugoslavia as elsewhere, the new generation of students were stirring. "I regard Bob Dylan," wrote one in *Vjesnik*, "as far more of a revolutionary than our fathers, so happy and proud with their bourgeois comforts and Mercedes cars." In June 1968 came a chance clash in Belgrade between students and the police, following which the students started a sit-in strike. "Workers, we are with you!" ran their slogans, displayed side by side with portraits of Marx and Tito. "Down with the Red Bourgeoisie." "Sack the politicians!" "Fewer cars, more schools!" While the authorities were debating what to do, Tito, with his usual sense of timing, suddenly appeared on television. He was, he announced, on the side of the students. The Government was at fault. Ministers must review their policies, get the economy moving, and help the lower paid workers. "If I am not capable of solving these problems," he concluded, "I have no business to be where I am." That night the strike was called off and delighted students danced the *kolo* in the streets of Belgrade. Tito, you found, if you talked to them, was more popular than ever.

But now, while the Yugoslavs sought to solve their own problems after their own fashion, came disturbing events elsewhere. On the night of 20–21 August 1968, without warning, the Soviet army occupied Prague. Tito, who from the first had welcomed Alexander Dubček's attempt to give Czech Communism a human face, immediately condemned the Soviet Government's action. "The entry of foreign military units into Czechoslovakia, without invitation or consent by the legal government," he said, "has given us cause for grave concern. The sovereignty of a socialist country has been violated and trampled underfoot and a serious blow struck at socialist and progressive forces worldwide."

It was clearly quite possible that, having successfully brought the Czechs back into line, the Kremlin might seek to apply the same treatment to Yugoslavia and indeed Roumania, also showing unwelcome signs of independence. Next day a resolution from the Central Committee of the Party left no doubt as to Yugoslavia's attitude in such an event. "Today, as always," it ran, "we are resolved to use all our forces and means to defend our independence, our revolution, and our own way of socialist development." No less significant, at a secret meeting with Tito two days later, President Ceaucescu of Roumania likewise committed himself to join in military action in the event of a Soviet attack.

None of this had passed unnoticed in Moscow. On 30 August the Soviet ambassador delivered to Tito personally a threatening note complaining of Yugoslavia's "unfriendly attitude." Tito's reaction was characteristic. Glancing through the note, he rang for his *chef de cabinet*. "Show him out," he said, as the ambassador sought to elaborate on its contents. "I will not be spoken to like that by anyone." "And you can tell your people in Moscow," he added as Comrade Benediktov left the room, "that if they come anywhere near us, we will fight them for twenty years."

That Tito meant what he said and was speaking not only for the Government, but for the people of Yugoslavia, was obvious to anyone in Belgrade at the time. There could be no mistaking their mood. "You won't need a parachute this time," said a friend to the present author, "you'll be here when it starts." From 21 August onward vast crowds surged through

the streets of Belgrade, cheering the Czechs, booing the Russians, singing national songs, and breaking every now and then into a *kolo*, the solemn yet triumphant measure, which can at one and the same time be a war dance, a funeral dance, a celebration of victory, or a mixture of all three. But no Soviet invasion came. Once again Tito, by timely and determined action, had averted a threat to his country's independence.

Alexander Dubček's attempt to "give Communism a human face" did not find favor with the Russians, who ruthlessly suppressed it. By making it clear to the Kremlin that he would fight if invaded, Tito ensured that the same treatment was not applied to him.

For a time the effect of the Czech crisis on Yugoslavia was unifying and astringent. The doctrine which Brezhnev had formulated to justify his action against Czechoslovakia could quite clearly be applied to Yugoslavia and might still be so applied if the circumstances were favorable. While in 1969 the Ninth Party Congress went some way to meet the demand for more freedom and greater autonomy within the Federation, the general feeling was that the Party must still retain a considerable measure of control. This was one intention behind the creation of a new Executive Bureau of the Party composed of two representatives from each of the republics and one from each of the two autonomous areas, with Tito himself as chairman. On the Government side, a corresponding presidium, also under Tito's chairmanship, was likewise designed to transfer the presidential functions to a collective leadership after his death. "Do you think it will work?" Tito asked the present author. "I don't see why not," I replied. "Nor do I," he said cheerfully.

And now the need for greater control was dramatically demonstrated by the reemergence in acute form of the old problem of the nationalities. Many people believed that this had been largely overcome during the war, when Partisans from all over Yugoslavia fought side by side, and had finally been resolved after the war by the introduction of a federal constitution. They were wrong. As the latest measures of liberalization and decentralization began to take effect, the differences in living standards between the regions became a serious cause of jealousy and friction. In the south the Macedonians did not see why they should live worse than the more advanced and possibly harder-working Croats and Slovenes in the north. Nor did the Croats and Slovenes necessarily see why they should subsidize their, according to them, less provident comrades in the south. Serbs and Croats, too, were often at odds. There were disputes over the disposal of foreign currency earnings and the allocation of investment funds and also over linguistic and cultural issues, all adding fuel to the latent fires of nationalism.

By the spring of 1970 the problem had become acute, particularly in Croatia where, despite painful memories of the Ustaše, there had been a regular resurgence of Croat nationalism, especially among the younger generation.

Early in 1971 abusive exchanges between the Serb and Croat Communist parties reached such a pitch that Tito himself was obliged to intervene. Summoning the Party Presidium to Brioni, he stressed the need for restraint, adding that Brezhnev had actually telephoned to offer him Soviet "fraternal assistance" should it be needed.

But in Croatia "national euphoria," as it was called, continued to gain strength. Bakarić, after many years at the helm, had now been joined in the leadership by three younger colleagues, the attractive and ambitious Savka Dapčević-Kučar, now prime minister, Miko Tripalo, the Party Secretary, and Pero Pirker, a former mayor of Zagreb, all inclined to play the nationalist card as a means of gaining popularity. Under their auspices support for "the national mass movement" increased by leaps and bounds both inside the Party and out and the membership of *Matica Hrvatska*, a Croat cultural fellowship with strong political overtones, jumped in a few months from two to forty thousand. The situation was fast getting out of hand.

In July Tito summoned the Party leaders to meet him in Zagreb. "You will see," he said, "that I am very angry." Nationalism, he told them, was running wild. Did they want a repetition of 1941? Again he spoke of the external danger and of Brezhnev's offer of help. "Others," he said, "are watching. Don't you realize they'd be here in a trice if disorders were to break out?...I demand firm action." He left them, or so he thought, in a chastened frame of mind.

In September, when he next visited Zagreb, an excited crowd of several hundred thousand Croats, feeling that, as a Croat, he must be on their side, turned out to cheer him and the Party leaders with him. He was delighted and said so. But in fact he had been misled. The Croat leaders, playing as usual to the gallery, were being carried along on a floodtide of nationalism which they made no attempt to check.

Returning from abroad in November, Tito quickly grasped that things in Croatia had gone dangerously far. On 22 November, after a number of inflammatory speeches by their leaders, the Zagreb students came out on strike, seeking at he same time to provoke a general strike and force a confrontation with the Government. The Party leaders, by now seriously worried, sought to reason with them, but in vain. Realizing the danger, Tito now summoned the Croat Party leaders to his hunting lodge at Karadjordjevo in Serbia, where they were later joined by the rest of the Presidium. Next day his statement to them was broadcast to the nation. The Croat leaders, he said, had pandered to nationalists and separatists. They were guilty of "rotten liberalism" in the face of what was fast becoming counterrevolution. It was intolerable that they should represent Croatia's grievances, however genuine, as national problems or seek to solve them by illegal means. It was equally intolerable that they should question the right of the Party Presidium to intervene in their affairs. It existed for that purpose. The Croat Central Committee must at once put their house in order.

The Croat Central Committee met in Zagreb on 12 December. The leaders of the Students' Federation had been arrested at dawn. Helmeted riot police occupied strategic points in the city. Helicopters hovered overhead. The army stood by. The resignation of Dapčević-Kučar, Tripalo, and Pirker was offered and accepted. Bakarić spoke blandly of "the political maturity which so facilitated the solution of little local difficulties" and the proceedings were brought to a dignified conclusion. Once again, the situation had been saved by Yugoslavia's eighty-year-old President.

Having demonstrated the virtues of "democratic centralism" in Croatia, Tito, determined as always to keep a proper balance, turned his attention to Serbia. Here there appeared to be too great an accumulation of financial power, lending substance to stories of Serbian hegemony. His answer was to purge the local Party leadership. Meeting them in October 1972 he found them at first reluctant to go—"lacking," as he put it, "in the virtue of self-criticism." But these difficulties were quickly overcome and a couple of weeks later it was announced that the resignations of the Party chairman and secretary had duly been offered and accepted. Two years later the invaluable principle of "democratic centralism" was formally embodied in a new federal constitution which gave the Party chairman a place as of right in the machinery of government.

For a time, following the Czech crisis, Soviet-Yugoslav relations remained cool. Every improvement was followed by a fresh falling out. Though Brezhnev, when in Yugoslavia in 1971, spoke dismissively of his own doctrine and specifically denied that he had any intention of marching into the Balkans, the possibility of a Soviet attack remained in people's minds and Yugoslavia's new system of "Total National Defense," especially instituted by parliament in February 1969, was clearly designed to meet such a threat.

During the nineteen-seventies Yugoslav relations with the West improved. An agreement with the European Economic Community made her economically less dependent on the Eastern bloc. The establishment of full diplomatic relations with the Vatican was important both internally and externally. In September 1971 Tito played host, not only to Mr. Brezhnev, but also to the President of the United States, whose visit he returned shortly afterward, bringing back with him promises of increased American help and investment.

Earlier that summer, the Yugoslav foreign minister, much to the indignation of the now violently anti-Chinese Russians, had visited China, until recently hostile to Yugoslavia, and heard his country praised for so resolutely defending her independence. At Lusaka a conference of nonaligned countries showed that Tito's much cherished concept of nonalignment was still alive, though two years later the renewed outbreak of hostilities in the Middle East found Yugoslavia once again closely aligned with the Soviet Union.

But as usual Tito did not take long to restore the balance. At the Tenth Party Congress in May 1974 he went out of his way to stress, in the presence of a top-level Soviet delegation, his Party's complete independence and Yugoslavia's absolute right to find her own way to Socialism. Just before the thirtieth victory anniversary celebrations held in Belgrade in May 1975, an article by Marshal Grechko, the Soviet minister of defense, claimed that there had been virtually no resistance in Yugoslavia during the war and that Yugoslavia had been liberated by the Bulgarians. This produced an indignant outburst from Tito. Nor were the heavily decorated Soviet marshals and generals who attended the parade very warmly received.

For Tito, now well into his eighties and still amazingly active, the international occasions he attended had a way of becoming personal triumphs. At the Helsinki Conference of European States in 1975, he was in many ways the dominant personality, while the fact that the powers assembled there met, in theory at any rate, on a basis of equality was in a sense a breakthrough for his ideas.

Another such occasion was the Conference of European

Tito in his study (right). *The painting in the background (reproduced in color on pages 20–21) meant much to him, representing his own struggle with a much stronger enemy.*

Tito's army (below) *formed a bulwark that enabled him to maintain a determined attitude toward Moscow. In a critical situation he said to the Soviet ambassador: "And you can tell your people in Moscow that if they come anywhere near us, we will fight them for twenty years."*

Communist Parties held in East Berlin in the summer of 1976, when he took advantage of the presence of the Soviet and other European Party leaders to reassert in the plainest terms his doctrine of different roads to Socialism and equality between Parties.

A year later, in May 1977, Tito celebrated his eighty-fifth birthday. It was marked by nationwide displays of genuine affection and enthusiasm. At his side throughout the celebrations was Jovanka, his wife of twenty-five years, gracious, smiling, and affectionate. Barely a month after this she made what turned out to be her last public appearance in his company. When that summer Tito set out on a highly successful series of visits to the Soviet Union, North Korea, and China, which he skillfully used to extol the benefits of ideological independence, she did not accompany him. Nor was she with him when he later visited America. By now her absence had aroused the interest of the foreign press. Nor did an announcement that the President's relations with his wife were his own business did nothing to help. Rumors of all kinds began to circulate that she had interfered in politics or even that there was another, younger woman in his life. In the end Tito explained that Jovanka simply got on his nerves. She was, it was said, living in seclusion at his villa in Dedinje. What had really happened remained obscure.

For some years doubts had been growing in the West about the Nonaligned Movement which its conferences at Algiers and Colombo did nothing to dispel. In the autumn of 1979 the conference of nonaligned countries held in Cuba under the aegis of Fidel Castro seemed to confirm the view that it was now firmly aligned on the side of the Soviet Union. An attempt by Tito to restore the balance was only partly successful.

Tito's faith in the Nonaligned Movement was, however, dramatically vindicated a few months later by the reactions of its members to the Soviet invasion of Afghanistan, which the great majority, including Yugoslavia, wholeheartedly condemned, both individually and at the United Nations. The Afghan crisis fulfilled another purpose. Nearly twelve years after the Soviet invasion of Czechoslovakia, there had been a tendency to forget the Brezhnev Doctrine. The Soviet attack on Afghanistan served as a salutary reminder of the reality of the Soviet threat to any country which could be considered to fall within an ever widening Soviet sphere of interest.

That Yugoslavia came within this category was all too clear. Tito was already seriously ill at this time. Coinciding with his illness, the Afghan crisis made Yugoslavia the center of worldwide concern. For the Kremlin to attempt a takeover would in the circumstances have been a decidedly risky undertaking.

His private life was, in his later years, a haven which Tito must often have hoped for in the hard times before and during the war. His twenty-five years with Jovanka (right) were on the whole happy. He enjoyed the pleasures of life, his friendships and his hobbies, and above all his family.

Until the very end of his life Tito continued to give an impression of exceptional mental and physical vigor. His zest for life remained undiminished. He worked hard, but not too hard, taking pleasure in eating well, dressing well, and living in agreeable surroundings. On his finger he continued to wear the handsome diamond ring he had bought with the rubles he had earned in Moscow before the war. Everything interested him. With any new acquisition, particularly anything mechanical, he was like a child with a new toy. As always, he possessed the happy gift of being able to set aside the cares of state and throw himself wholeheartedly into some sparetime hobby or pursuit, tending his vines, working with his lathe, riding, watching a movie, shooting, or swimming. Round him in the country or by the sea he enjoyed having his family and his wartime friends. He was above all careful never to let himself become isolated. On his travels through Yugoslavia, he made a point of talking to as many people as he could from every walk of life and listening to what they had to say.

With the years his outlook, never narrow, widened still further and his sense of humor became even stronger. As a man he became mellower and more human. But he never for a moment lost his basic toughness and shrewdness, remaining to the end as alert, as decisive, and as hard-headed as ever and as ready as ever to face resolutely, realistically, and ruthlessly any situation that might confront him.

When, after a protracted illness, Tito was borne to his grave, the world paid its respects at his graveside.

Below: *His wife, Jovanka.*

Next page: *The great leaders, from left to right: Soviet chief of state Brezhnev; U.S. Vice President Mondale and President Carter's mother, Lillian; Chinese party chief Hua Guofeng.*

Overleaf: *A nation in pain and mourning.*

Tito died after a long, hard-fought illness at the beginning of May 1980, only a few days short of his eighty-eighth birthday. A year or two earlier he had entertained the young Prince of Wales at his villa at Igalo in Montenegro. The atmosphere was relaxed and friendly and Tito talked freely of his long life. "If you could have it over again," asked Prince Charles, "would you want it any different?" "No," said Tito.

"A lot of it was very tough, but I would still want it the way it was." It was the answer of a man who all his life had been a fighter and remained one to the end.

To the now dwindling band of those who had served with him during the war Tito's funeral, which was held in Belgrade, brought back, as it was bound to, memories, some painful, some glorious, of those epic years. It left them, as it left the ordinary people of Yugoslavia who turned out in their millions to pay him a final tribute, with a sense of personal loss.

Attended by kings, presidents, and heads of government from more than a hundred and twenty different countries, the ceremony was first and foremost a military one. To a salute of twenty-one guns, the coffin, covered with the Yugoslav tricolor, was carried by eight guards officers from the Parliament Building, where it had lain in state, to a plain gun-carriage. On this, while jet fighters screeched overhead, it was drawn slowly between immense crowds, along the Knez

Miloša, and up the hill to Dedinje. With the coffin marched three generals, carrying the Marshal's decorations and medals. At the head of the funeral procession the colors of the original Partisan Brigades were carried, not by the veterans, but by young men as ready as their fathers and grandfathers to fight for their country's independence. Next came the little group of National Heroes, elderly men and women, wearing round their necks the red-and-white ribbon and golden badge of the highest Partisan award for gallantry in action.

anthem of long ago, now discarded by the Kremlin in favor of other, less subversive melodies, and then *Hej Sloveni*, for Yugoslavs likewise a call to rebellion and revolt. Foremost among the mourners at the graveside, along with Tito's sons Žarko and Mišo and their families, stood his widow Jovanka, overcome with grief, the estrangement of recent years thus finally brought to an end.

At Tito's funeral his two official successors, Lazar Koliševski, the new President, and Stevan Doronjski, the new Party

At Dedinje in the grounds of the suburban villa where he had lived since the war and only a few hundred yards from that villa, where he had hidden out in the fateful summer of 1941, Tito was laid to rest under a plain white marble tombstone, inscribed in gold letters with his name and the years of his birth and death. A volley was fired an then, while kings, presidents, and prime ministers stood to attention, a military brass band played with solemn emphasis, first the *Internationale*, that mournful, yet somehow exultant revolutionary

Chairman, both delivered formal speeches of eulogy. But, though formal, their speeches left no doubts whatever on one score: his fellow countrymen's absolute determination to hold to the course he had set and to defend against all comers their hard-won independence, their national unity, and their own Yugoslav brand of socialism. Points which cannot have been wasted on Leonid Brezhnev, who, though in poor health, had made the long journey from Moscow to pay his last respects to a revolutionary so very different from himself.

EPILOGUE

If ever there was a child of the twentieth century, it was Josip Broz, born eight years before it began, the son of a poor Croat peasant, suddenly to become famous some fifty years later as Marshal Tito of Yugoslavia. Our century's blood-stained landmarks, two World Wars, the Russian Revolution, the Spanish Civil War, the emergence of Stalin, Hitler, and Mussolini, the great Soviet purges of the thirties, the assassinations at Sarajevo and Marseilles, all played their part in his development and had their impact on his career. And he, in his turn, made his impact on the century.

The two go together, the man and the age. The former, it can be said, was symbolic of the latter. And this, in a sense, is encouraging. For Tito was a rebel. And a rebel, in an age of mass production and power blocs and monolithic systems of government, is a healthy phenomenon. Nor is it really surprising that Tito should have been a rebel. He was a Yugoslav and Yugoslavs are natural rebels, stubborn, proud, and irrepressible, ready to die, or to kill, for an idea.

The storms Tito weathered would have destroyed a lesser man. He rode each in turn and each carried him a stage further on his way. The First World War taught him to fight and then took him as a prisoner to Russia, where the Revolution made him a revolutionary. When the Yugoslav police jailed him, he used his time in jail to educate himself. Stalin's purges, which wiped out so many of his comrades, left him

A gallery of portraits extending over sixty years of his life.

118

Secretary of the Yugoslav Communist Party so that the Second World War found him at the head of an efficient underground organization, ready to be turned into a formidable resistance movement.

The war gave Tito his chance. Within four years he had freed his own country by his own efforts and those of his fellow-countrymen. At the head of a powerful military and political machine which he had himself created, he was then well able to resist the attempts of his former Soviet sponsors to reduce him to satellite status. Courageous, resolute, clear-thinking and, when necessary, completely ruthless, he steered his country through one postwar crisis after another with the same sure touch and steady nerves that during four years of war had enabled him, against overwhelming odds, to carry his perpetually outgunned and outnumbered forces through to ultimate victory.

By the military chroniclers Tito will be remembered as a great guerrilla leader. In the judgment of history he is likely to bulk still larger for his stand against Stalin and its impact on world Communism. Until 1948 Soviet power had been securely based on the absolute authority and infallibility of the Kremlin. Tito challenged both and survived. The fact of his survival pointed a moral and exerted an influence which were to extend far beyond the frontiers of his own country and the span of his lifetime. It showed, for all to see, what a small

His homeland, the lovely but not very fertile Zagorje and the village of Kumrovec, was dear to Tito his whole life long. He said that the local sayings and tales about folk heroes, such as Matija Gubec, made a deep impression on him as a youth.

country, well-led, courageous, and independent-minded, could do. The events of 1948 and the results that flowed from them marked a turning point in history.

Tito with his dog Lux, which saved its master's life. This occurred during an air attack on 9 June 1943. A bomb splinter, which came close to hitting Tito, killed the dog which threw itself across the head of Tito as he lay on the ground. Also killed in this raid were his companions, his bodyguard Djuro Vujović and Captain Stuart, a British liaison officer.

For Yugoslavia Tito's death signified the end of an era, which had started four decades earlier with the epic years of Partisan resistance and continued after the war with thirty-five years of stoutly sustained independence. That Tito's own personality and force of character played a decisive part in the events of these forty years is indisputable. But Tito could not have done what he did without the support of the Yugoslav people. A typical Yugoslav, his indomitable courage, independent spirit, steady nerves, and intense national pride found from the first a ready echo in the ordinary Yugoslav man in the street or on the hillside.

This augurs well for the future. No less than Tito, the Yugoslav people value the country he helped them build up from the wreckage of the war years, the high standard of living he enabled them to attain, and the independence he helped them to preserve and are as determined as he was to defend them.

After Tito what? This is a question the world has been asking for many years. I put it to Tito when he was in his late fifties. "Come back in twenty years and I'll tell you," he replied. Just twenty years later I reminded him of his promise. This time I found him ready enough to discuss the question of his succession. It would have been unlike him to neglect it. The answer he found lay not in one man (potential candidates lacked his durability), but rather in a collective leadership which, as Tito himself said publicly some years later, seemed the best way of avoiding a scramble for power and the dangers attendant on it.

For a number of years before Tito's death this collective leadership had in fact been governing the country. Officially, presidential power, in both Party and Government, resided in a Presidium giving due representation to the six republics and two autonomous regions of the federation. For practical purposes it was concentrated in the hands of a kind of inner cabinet, also carefully balanced ethnically, who for some time had been taking most day-to-day decisions without reference to Tito and only consulting him on major questions of policy. Tito will nevertheless inevitably be missed on two scores. First for what he represented in the eyes of the ordinary people of Yugoslavia. And secondly as a world statesman who could talk on equal terms to any of the world leaders.

It is conceivable that at some future time Yugoslavia will again throw up a comparable figure. At the moment there is no obvious candidate for the job. What is more important is

that there are at the head of affairs half a dozen or more hard-headed, able, experienced men, determined to keep their country on the course which, with their help, she has been following for a number of years past.

Though Yugoslavia possesses a single-party system, this does not mean that there is not a lively and continuing public debate on a wide range of subjects between genuinely conflicting interests, the interests, that is, of different regions and different sections of the community and economy, all requiring to be satisfied before a consensus can be arrived at. It is not parliamentary democracy, as the West understands it, but in its own way it works.

The same can be said of Yugoslavia's unique economic system. "We are no longer dogmatists," Tito said to me six or seven years ago. "We are concerned with making things work." And there can be no doubt that, after its own fashion, the Yugoslav economy does work. Numerous books have been written about its system of independent self-managing enterprises. Certainly one of its virtues is that it is not over-centralized. (There are no state industries.) It leaves scope for initiative and enterprise and encourages them with adequate rewards. And it takes proper account of the needs of the consumer.

Decentralization is also the solution that has been found for the still potentially thorny problem of the nationalities.

New Year's Eve celebration: Jovanka and Tito, 31 December 1967.

Under the present federal, indeed practically confederal system, the six national republics and two autonomy regions are in practice self-governing for all purposes except foreign affairs and defense. In fact it can be said that a greater degree of autonomy would amount to independence. To any rational person (though nationalists are not always rational) it is a system that successfully avoids any suggestion of the Serbian hegemony that was the curse of the old Yugoslavia. Moreover, by a sensible system of mutual economic aid and cooperation, much has been done to overcome the dangerous differences which still persist between republics in their respective levels of economic development and prosperity.

In any one of these contexts one is constantly reminded how lucky the Yugoslavs have been to have had a man of Tito's caliber at the head of affairs for close on forty years, in fact, for two thirds of the sixty years since Yugoslavia first came into being. It gave him time to endow their country with a stability and a sense of direction which even twenty years ago would have seemed impossible. The last ten years, in particular, have been marked by solid progress in these respects. Less than a decade ago the problem of the nationalities was still a dangerous one which demanded (and received) drastic treatment from Tito personally. As elsewhere the younger generation were at that time more restless and feckless than today. In the last ten years a new, more responsive and responsible generation of teenagers and twenty-year-olds has emerged, more committed, more conscious of being Yugoslavs, and more determined to carry on the tradition of their fathers and grandfathers who, after fighting to free their country from the Germans, toiled to rebuild it after the war. Nor is it only the younger generation who have become more Yugoslav-minded. Gone are the days when Tito (like King Alexander before him) could complain what he was the only Yugoslav in the country. Thirty or forty more years of intermarriage between races already closely akin to each other, better communications, and more education have all had their effect. Even Belgrade, for so long a symbol of Serbian hegemony, is fast becoming a Yugoslav city and a proper federal capital.

It would be idle to pretend that no one in Yugoslavia is concerned about a possible external threat. In 1980 Tito's illness and the Soviet invasion of Afghanistan both reminded the Yugoslavs of their exposed position. But an external threat has always served to unite Serbs, Croats, and Slovenes and once again it produced this effect. Even with Tito gone, Yugoslavs face the future with steadiness and confidence and are as determined as ever to maintain their country's independence. Independence, they emphasize, not only of one, but of both power blocs, East and West.

Certainly their well-led, well-trained, and well-equipped

army of more than a quarter of a million men plus territorial reserves said to amount to three million more, specially trained to fight a prolonged war of resistance, inspire abundant confidence. Yugoslavia also has a competent and vigilant security service. But perhaps an even better guarantee against the danger of subversion is that in Yugoslavia too many people have too good a life and, in the widest sense, too much to lose, to want to see their country disappear behind the Iron Curtain.

"Whatever the future holds in store, this much is certain. For his early plots and stratagems, for his leadership in the War of National Liberation, in those three and a half years of bitter strife, and, last but not least, for his stubborn defiance of the Kremlin and resolute rejection of Stalin's overlordship, Tito, like Tsar Lazar and Kara Djordje before him, will always be remembered in the history and legend of his own people. A typical South Slav, if ever there was one, his fame will be celebrated by future generations of South Slavs, the fame of his virtues and of his vices alike."

FROM "DISPUTED BARRICADE" BY FITZROY MACLEAN

123

As the dead body of their President and national hero Tito made the long trip from Ljubljana, capital of Slovenia, to Belgrade, capital of the Federation, the train stopped at many stations along the line.

On all these stops a song was sung by the assembled crowd, which seemed to be a litany, and a vow:

Druže Tito ljubičice bela,
pozdravlja te omladina cela,
pozdravlja te i staro i mlado,
druže Tito ti narodno nado;
druže Tito mi ti se kunemo
da sa tvoga puta ne skrenemo.

Comrade Tito, our white lily,
All the young are greeting you,
All the young and all the old,
Comrade Tito, your people's hope:
Comrade Tito, to you we swear,
From your path never to stray.

PICTURE CREDITS

Bildarchiv Bucher, Lucerne: 94

Bildarchiv Handke, Bad Berneck: 14 (bottom right)

Bilderdienst Süddeutscher Verlag, Munich: 14 (top, bottom left); 15; 32; 40 (right); 42 (top); 100; 100/101; 101

Contact Press, Paris: 115 (left)

Die Wildente, Hamburg: 41

Ivo Eterović, Belgrade: 112; 113; 122 (top, bottom row: 2nd from left and 2nd from right); 123 (left and right)

Euprapress, Munich: 104 (bottom center)

Fototanjug, Belgrade: 5; 29 (below); 30 (left); 62; 66; 73; 81; 85; 87; 102 (top); 104 (2nd from top, bottom left and right); 106/107; 111; 123 (2nd from left)

Gamma, Paris (Photo: Alain Mingam): 115 (center)

Gamma, Paris (Photo: Christian Vioujard): 110; 114 (left)

Globus, Zagreb: 10/11; 11 (top, below right); 12 (left); 121 (above)

Keystone Press, Zurich: 58 (left); 96/97; 108

The Mansell Collection, London (Photo: E.O. Hoppé): 26 (top)

Muzej Revolucije, Belgrade: 31 (bottom); 37; 50; 77 (bottom left and right); 78 (top); 82 (top); 118 (bottom left); 119 (bottom row: center and 2nd from right); 120 (bottom row: left, 2nd from left, 3rd from left, 3rd from right and 2nd from right)

John Philips, New York: 83 (right); 114 (right)

Photo Oriol, Paris: 34 (center, right)

Photopress, Zurich: 35 (center right); 58 (top); 59 (bottom); 120 (bottom right)

Publisher's Archives, Lucerne: 18 (center, bottom)

Ringier Bilderdienst, Zurich: 35 (center and bottom); 40 (left); 79 (center); 115 (right); 116/117

Toni Schneiders, Lindau: 25 (bottom)

Yugoslav Review, Belgrade: 3; 9; 10 (top right); 22 (bottom); 34 (left); 34/35; 78 (2nd row right); 78/79; 104 (top, 2nd from bottom); 119 (above, bottom left); 121 (below left and right); 122 (below left, center and right); 123 (2nd from right); 124

PICTURE CREDITS FROM PUBLISHED WORKS

FOURTEEN CENTURIES OF STRUGGLE FOR FREEDOM, Military Museum of Belgrade: 60/61; 65 (center); 67; 68 (left); 69; 72 (left); 76 (right)

Franz Hubmann: K.U.K. FAMILIENALBUM, Die Welt von gestern in 319 Photographien, Fritz Molden Verlag, Vienna: 10 (below)

Gustav Krklec et al.: JOSIP BROZ TITO, Spektar, Zagreb 1977: 2; 20/21; 78 (2nd row left)

Fitzroy Maclean: DISPUTED BARRICADE, Jonathan Cape, London 1957: 58 (below); 96

Dragan Marković and Tihomir Stanojević: TITO, HIS LIFE AND WORK, Stvarnost, Zagreb 1963: 6; 6/7; 8; 10 (top left); 13; 16; 16/17; 26 (bottom); 27; 28; 29 (top); 30 (right); 31 (top); 35 (center left); 36; 38; 39; 42 (below); 43; 44; 45; 44/45; 46; 47; 48; 49; 51; 52; 53; 54; 56; 57; 59 (top, center); 60; 61; 63; 64 (left); 76 (left); 77 (above left and right); 78 (bottom left and right); 79 (above left and right); 80 (top); 82 (bottom); 83 (bottom); 84 (left); 86; 88/89; 89; 90/91; 93; 95; 98/99; 99; 102/103; 102 (bottom); 106; 118 (top, bottom row: 2nd from left, 2nd from right, right); 119 (bottom 2nd from left and right); 120 (top)

MLADOST JOSIPA BROZA, Mladost, Belgrade: 19 (center, bottom)

Kosta Nadj: RAPORTI VRHOVNOM KOMANDANTU, Spektar, Zagreb 1979: 55

Footnotes (for page 71)

* It has been suggested that Tito's now famous stratagem was in fact more of a last-minute improvisation. That it succeeded is, however, indisputable.

* At the height of the Fourth Offensive Tito had authorized talks with the Germans regarding a possible further exchange of prisoners and the future treatment of wounded. They were conducted by Milovan Djilas and Koča Popović and were wider in scope than was for many years officially admitted, touching on belligerent status for the Partisans and a possible truce. In the event, however, the only agreement reached concerned a limited exchange of prisoners. Any question of a truce or indeed of belligerent status for the Partisans was, in any case, soon to become academic in the extreme.

Left: Resistance monument in Valjevo; see also page 5.

INDEX